FEEL…DEAL…HEAL…

Acquiring Love: Liberty Over Vulnerable Emotions

Dr. Latoshia Daniels

Copyright © 2024 Dr. Latoshia Daniels

ISBN: 979-8-869334-77-0

Table of Contents

DEDICATION

In loving memory of my precious son, DeUnte.
Though you are no longer with us, your love continues to inspire me.
Your memory will forever be a source of strength and motivation.
I dedicate this work to you with eternal love and
cherished memories. You are 4E Ma's boy.

ACKNOWLEDGEMENTS

To My Lord and Savior Jesus Christ. Thank you, Sir, for giving me the tools necessary to write this book. Thank you for guiding me on the journey. Thank you for showing me how to love me. Father, please breathe life into this book.

To my incredible husband and best friend, Tank. You are the chapter that brought light, love, and unwavering support into the pages of life when I needed it the most. Your boundless kindness and understanding have been a beacon of hope, guiding me through the darkest of times. You never judged me or defined me by the challenges I faced when you entered my world. Instead, you saw the person beyond the circumstances, the strength within the struggle, and the love that knows no boundaries. Thank you for loving me for me. For seeing me and for choosing me. TNT for life.

To my beloved sons, in the face of adversity, you did not give up on me; you gave me hope. Your resilience and compassion taught me the true meaning of family and perseverance. You reminded me that love is the constant that can weather any storm. I love you all more than I could even express in words or actions. Thank you all for being awesome children and trusting me during tough times in our lives.

To my dearest family and treasured friends, during a life-altering storm that has spanned over four challenging years, your unwavering support continues to be my guiding light and refuge. Your presence, love, and belief in me are the constants that provide solace amid uncertainty. Thank you for not giving up on me. Thank you for knowing who I am and standing firm on that which you know to be true.

ABOUT THE AUTHOR

Dr. Latoshia Daniels is a wife, mother, emerging author, speaker, trainer, coach and entrepreneur. She is dedicated to helping others to become the best version of themselves. She is the author of Level Up: Gaining Power During the Fight. She is the founder of Links of Love (L.O.L.), a nonprofit that aims to empower and mentor youth and young adults. Dr. Daniels graduated from Walden University, where she received a Doctor of Social Work degree. She obtained her Master of Social Work and Bachelor of Arts in Criminal Justice from the University of Arkansas at Little Rock. Dr. Latoshia worked as a Licensed Clinical Social worker for over 13 years before a major storm swept through and changed the trajectory of her life. She has an intentional agenda of combining the Word of God with her clinical knowledge in mental and behavioral health to help others heal from emotional wounds and overcome life's woes. Dr. Latoshia's desire is to aid others with not just being survivors but healed survivors who thrive and get in a position where they can receive all God has for them. She gives God all the glory for the favor that is upon her life. Love is her motive.

INTRODUCTION

Greetings,

Welcome to "Feel-Deal-Heal: Acquiring LOVE – Liberty Over Vulnerable Emotions." I pray this book will help you find or reclaim your joy. "Feel-Deal-Heal" is a personal exploration into increasing emotional intelligence while being the process of healing from emotional wounds. As humans, we feel a range of emotions. How we feel often impacts our interactions with others, decision-making, and even our self-perception. Many of us try to avoid feeling emotions that make us feel vulnerable or uncomfortable. So, you do the Heisman on them and keep pushing forward. What many fail to recognize is by ignoring emotional discomfort, you are contributing to a much larger problem. Before you know it, you are carrying around emotional baggage that weighs you down or emotional chains that hold you bound, or you build a wall of protection, but it blocks out the good and causes you to be misunderstood. As a result, you become resentful, intolerable, distrustful, and more.

"Feel-Deal-Heal" was conceived during a hellish time in my life. Sitting inside a cold jail cell, I searched for a way to make sense of my distress, pain, and turmoil. The search led me to my foundation, my Lord and Savior, Jesus Christ. He showed me that I had to die to myself for Him to save, heal, renew, and restore me. So, through my process of breaking with the use of my clinical skills, I learned to FEEL emotions that I once avoided intentionally and unintentionally. I began to DEAL with the situations contributing to the feelings, and then I began to HEAL. I embraced the love mindset and acquired L.O.V.E. – (L)iberty (O)ver (V)ulnerable (E)motions.

"Feel-Deal-Heal" serves as my heartfelt message to you. It comprises a collection of compassionate insights aimed at helping you identify areas where emotional wounds linger, and where emotional barriers may have taken root, hindering your ability to heal and flourish. My goal is to assist you in starting the healing process from past or present emotional turmoil and enhancing your emotional intelligence (EQ) through the cultivation of a love mindset.

The LOVE Mindset empowers you to embrace your emotions while maintaining control over your emotional experiences. Throughout this journey, you'll explore your emotional patterns and experiences that may impede your sense of wholeness and happiness. You'll also gain insight into how your emotional well-being influences your relationships with others. I sincerely hope that this book will serve as a guiding light on your path to healing. May it not only facilitate emotional healing but also contribute to your spiritual growth and well-being.

Friends, life often presents us with challenging situations, and it's natural to experience emotional distress along the way. Many of us haven't learned how to effectively release the pain from hurtful experiences, so we end up carrying it with us. This book is your guide to lighten that load. We will talk about feeling those emotions, dealing with them smartly, and healing so you can live freely. It is about not letting tough feelings define you but using them as stepping stones towards a thriving life. I desire that you move from being a survivor of past adverse situations that left you emotionally distraught to being a healed survivor who thrives. Let's navigate this journey together. I encourage you to embrace the love mindset, acquire liberty over those vulnerable emotions, and ultimately overcome emotional pain to heal your wounds.

LOVE MINDSET

During the inception of my nonprofit organization, I found inspiration in the concept of love. Recognizing God as love, I began contemplating how applying love can enhance our mental, emotional, and spiritual well-being. Working with clients in a clinical setting, I realized the crucial role of

Love (God) in attaining liberation from mental and emotional barriers that hinder healthy progress. This realization gave birth to the LOVE Mindset, and since then, I've been striving to articulate it in a way that empowers others to embrace it and overcome life's challenges. This mindset helps individuals navigate uncomfortable emotions they often try to avoid or express inappropriately, fostering healing and growth.

The LOVE Mindset is an approach to life centered around fostering empathy, compassion, and understanding in all interactions. It involves prioritizing love as the guiding principle in thoughts, words, and actions, leading to greater harmony, fulfillment, and connection with oneself and others. By actively cultivating positive emotions in daily life, you and I can counteract the effects of negative emotions and promote emotional stability and healing over time.

The LOVE Mindset positively impacts mental wellness by promoting emotional resilience, fostering positive relationships, and enhancing self-compassion. When you adopt the love mindset, you prioritize empathy, kindness, grace, and forgiveness, which can reduce stress, anxiety, and depression. By cultivating a sense of connection and belonging with others, the LOVE Mindset provides support and validation, buffering against feelings of isolation and loneliness. Additionally, practicing self-compassion and acceptance allows you to navigate challenges more effectively and bounce back from setbacks. Overall, the LOVE Mindset promotes a holistic approach to mental wellness, nurturing emotional well-being, and promoting a sense of fulfillment and purpose in life.

VULNERABLE VS. NEGATIVE EMOTIONS

Oh, and just in case you are wondering what vulnerable emotions are, they are those feelings that make us feel a bit exposed or sensitive. These emotions include things like sadness, fear, or insecurity – anything that makes us feel a little fragile and limited. They are called "vulnerable" because they can leave us open to being more affected by what is going on around us. Understanding and navigating these vulnerable emotions is important for our well-being, as they often play a significant role in our responses to challenging situations. Another contributor to emotional pain is negative emotions, the cousin of vulnerable emotions. The two are related but not the same. Negative emotions encompass a broader range of feelings, including sadness, anger, fear, resentment, jealousy, isolation, and more. While many vulnerable emotions can be classified as negative, not all negative emotions necessarily make us feel vulnerable. Understanding both types of emotions is crucial for managing our responses to various situations and promoting emotional well-being.

Do you need healing? If you don't need to heal, maybe, this book will assist you with understanding the emotional reactions or responses of others who do. Therefore, you will become more compassionate. For those in need of healing let's begin to explore your junkie junk so that you can acquire L.O.V.E. by learning to feel...deal...heal... As you read this book and work through the companion journal. I encourage you to take your time. Don't rush your healing process. This book is not a substitute for seeking professional assistance. Having face-to-face interactions with a trained professional who can assist you with processing is an effective tool to help you heal appropriately. Dealing with painful or hurtful moments and experiences can be difficult. Especially if you have held onto the pain, hurt, anger, fear, resentment, unforgiveness, etc., for a long time.

I also encourage you to get a solid but healthy support system. Having someone you can share with and be vulnerable with is necessary for healthy living. Let those who love and care for you help you. I will talk more about this matter in a later letter. For now, inform your loved ones that you are about to journey down the road to healing by acquiring L.O.V.E. so that you will show up each day the person God created you to be and you will be healthy while doing it.

Are you ready to acquire L.O.V.E.? Are you excited about healing? Well, let's get started. I will see you on the next level.

May God bless you to have peace and a full recovery,

Dr. Latoshia

PS. It is often stated that music is a universal language. It has the remarkable ability to soothe, uplift, and accompany us through life's various chapters. As a coping skill, it serves as a powerful ally in navigating emotions and finding solace. Each note and lyric can resonate with our experiences, offering a therapeutic escape. During this journey listen to the song noted in each letter – let the melodies be your companion in moments of reflection, resilience, and joy. FYI every song is not from the gospel/Christian music genre. If you don't listen to secular music just skip the song.

*"In order to stop the cycle
of 'hurt people, hurting people,' we
must take the time to feel-deal-heal."*

-Dr. Latoshia

LETTER OF LOVE #1: EMOTIONS

Have you ever heard the song "Emotions" by H-Town? I may be telling my age, but the song was a hit. "Emotions make you cry sometimes. Emotions make you sad sometimes. Emotions make you glad sometimes. But most of all they make you fall in love."

Emotions are an inherent part of our human makeup, woven into the very fabric of our existence. They are the colorful part of us, giving texture to our interactions and allowing us to experience the full spectrum of the human condition. All humans have the capacity to express and feel emotions. Emotions, from the warmth of love to the sting of sorrow, provide depth and meaning to our lives. However, when faced with challenges or offenses, it becomes crucial to manage these emotions effectively. Just as a skilled fisherman steers a ship through stormy waters, we must navigate the tempestuous seas of our emotions with wisdom and self-awareness. By acknowledging and understanding our emotions, we can harness their power and transform them into catalysts for growth and resilience. Through emotional management, we develop the ability to respond thoughtfully rather than react impulsively, empowering ourselves to overcome obstacles and emerge stronger on the other side.

Ironically, societal opinions often present a contradictory narrative when it comes to emotions. While they are seen as an integral part of our humanity, a prevailing expectation of emotional suppression or detachment exists, especially in certain contexts. Society tends to view emotional vulnerability as a weakness, emphasizing the need for indifference and control. For example, when a male is told at a young age, "Boys don't cry," or the phrase "Don't let them see you sweat." These contradictory stances can lead to confusion and inner conflict as individuals grapple with the pressure to conform to societal expectations while also recognizing the importance of acknowledging and processing their emotions. However, it is essential to recognize that true strength lies in embracing our emotions rather than suppressing or denying them.

Emotional intelligence, often abbreviated as EQ, is our capacity to recognize, understand, manage, and harness our own emotions while also empathizing with and influencing the emotions of others. It encompasses a spectrum of skills, from self-awareness and self-regulation to empathy and effective interpersonal relationships. It is the blueprint that aids us with navigating the intricate web of human emotions, enabling individuals to communicate effectively, make sound decisions, build healthier relationships, and cultivate resilience in the face of life's challenges. It is not only a personal asset but a vital social skill that enhances our ability to connect with others, resolve conflicts, and lead with empathy and authenticity. It guides our ability to feel-deal-heal.

Emotional intelligence is a skill that must be taught and cultivated. Teaching emotional intelligence equips individuals with essential life skills that improve both personal and professional lives – relationships, effective communication, conflict resolution, mental health, self-awareness, leadership skills, adaptability, social awareness, and more. As I end this letter, I would like to leave you with some questions to assist you with exploring your emotional awareness. Please go to the Feel-Deal-Heal Journal and complete prompts for LOL #1.

Peace and Love,

Dr. Latoshia

PS. As you continue this journey, I dare you to get to know the God ordained you.

Song: "Cry" by Lyfe Jennings

Go to the Feel-Deal-Heal Journal and complete the writing prompt for LOL #1.

*"The Lord is near to the brokenhearted,
and saves the crushed in spirit"*

– Psalm 34:18.

Letter of Love #2: Knowledge Is Power

Greetings!

When topics pertaining to race, politics, and religion surface in conversation, do you become uncomfortable and raise your finger to exit the conversation? When the word mental health is mentioned, many people become uncomfortable. It's difficult to discuss a very important subject seriously because many remain ignorant on purpose or due to miseducation.

I want you to be informed correctly. Mental health is not a bad word or a bad thing. Good mental health is essential for overall well-being and quality of life. Mental health refers to a person's emotional, psychological, and social well-being. It encompasses emotional resilience, positive relationships, effective stress management, and overall psychological well-being. Good mental health implies a state of well-being in which you can function effectively, cope with life's challenges, and make meaningful contributions to society.

Mental illness, on the other hand, refers to a specific condition or disorder that affects a person's thoughts, emotions, behavior, or mental functioning. Mental illnesses can range from common disorders like depression and anxiety to more severe conditions like bipolar disorder or schizophrenia. They often require diagnosis and treatment by mental health professionals.

In summary, mental health is a broad concept related to well-being and quality of life, while mental illness is a specific condition that can disrupt mental health and impair your level of functioning. Good mental health is essential for leading a full life and reducing the risk of mental illness.

Knowledge is power. If you are struggling to regulate your mood, you feel hopeless, unmotivated, worthless, sleeping too much or not enough or sleep disturbance, crying spells, anger, inability to focus, pay attention to details, racing thoughts, swift changes in mood, suicidal ideations, changes in appetite, constant worry and it's been ongoing for more than two weeks, please my friend seek professional help. Undiagnosed or ineffective treatment of a mental illness can result in death. Please gain knowledge or remain knowledgeable so that you can participate in keeping yourself healthy spiritually, physically, mentally, and emotionally. Friends, it's okay to have Jesus and a therapist, counselor, or life coach.

Here's to good health,

Dr. Latoshia

PS. Knowledge is power; get in the know now!

Song: "Depression" by Dax

Go to the Feel-Deal-Heal Journal and complete the writing prompt for LOL #2.

"The heart of the discerning acquires knowledge, for the ears of the wise seek it out."

-Proverbs 18:15

Letter of Love # 3: Damaged Roots

Greetings,

How are you doing? You made it to your third letter of love. Are you going to stick with me? I am on this journey with you. Let's begin to dig a little deeper.

I must admit an embarrassing truth about myself. I am horrible with plants. I have come to accept that the art of growing beautiful plants remains elusive for me. I simply haven't been bestowed with a green thumb. While both my papa (biological father) and daddy (he who accepted me as his own flesh and blood) effortlessly cultivated flourishing houseplants and lush gardens, my attempts at nurturing greenery often ended with wilted leaves and frustrated sighs. My papa's plants were so beautiful and tranquil. My daddy had beautiful vegetable gardens. I loved the results the gardens produced, but as a child and teen, I hated the work involved in getting the delicious produce. Cultivating the soil and gathering the harvest were not easy tasks.

I know you do not know this about me, but I deeply enjoy eating watermelon. I mean, really, really, really enjoy watermelon. I was the watermelon-eating champion at summer camp for two years in a row. Camp Heart O Hill's Watermelon Eating Champion. Yep, that's me! Each summer, my family and I would discard the watermelon rims and seeds in the same location in the yard. One year, I noticed something sprouting up from the ground. OMG! It's a watermelon. I have a watermelon patch! The only hard work associated with growing the patch was walking outside to discard the rims, seeds, and juice after eating. I didn't cultivate the soil. There was no application of fertilizer.

I said all that to say that sometimes emotional damage may be the result of intentional or unintentional acts. Someone may purposefully or unintentionally say or do something to hurt you. A traumatic event or loss or less severe but negative circumstance happens. You don't have to do anything for it to occur, but you grab hold of the pain, and it takes root and begins to infect good roots and contribute to the production of toxic fruit or being fruitless.

Dealing with root issues is crucial when identifying and addressing emotional injuries. Just as a plant's health depends on the condition of its soil and roots, our emotional well-being is deeply connected to the underlying causes of our emotional distress. Surface-level symptoms may manifest as anger, sadness, anxiety, or other emotional reactions, but it is essential to dig deeper and uncover the root causes that contribute to these emotions. By addressing the root issues, we can achieve lasting healing and growth.

Identifying and dealing with root issues involves introspection and sometimes seeking professional help. It requires a willingness to explore our past experiences, traumas, belief systems, and patterns of thinking and behavior. By delving into the underlying factors contributing to our emotional injuries, we gain insight into our lives, triggers, and recurring themes. This process allows us to make connections between past experiences and current emotional responses, enabling us to break free from harmful patterns and develop healthier coping mechanisms. By dealing with root issues, we create a solid foundation for emotional well-being, paving the way for personal transformation and the cultivation of healthier relationships with ourselves and others.

Grow healthy,

Dr. Latoshia

Song: "Energy" by Keri Hilson

Go to the Feel-Deal-Heal Journal and complete the writing prompt for LOL #3.

"Guard against turning back from the grace of God.

Let no one become like a bitter plant that grows up and causes many troubles with its poison."

-Hebrews 12:15 GNT

LETTER OF LOVE #4: WHAT'S @ THE CORE?

Greetings!

The core of an apple serves as the central support structure for the entire fruit, providing stability and strength. It houses the seeds, which are essential for reproduction and the continuation of the apple species. The core also contains nutrients and fibers that contribute to the apple's nutritional value. Additionally, the core plays a crucial role in the apple's texture and flavor, influencing the crispness and sweetness of the fruit.

Like the core of an apple, core beliefs are the central foundation of an individual's values and principles. They provide stability and shape our worldview, guiding our decisions and actions. Just as the core of an apple houses seeds, core beliefs serve as the source of our thoughts and behaviors, influencing our growth and development. Additionally, like the core of an apple affecting its texture and flavor, core beliefs impact our identity and shape our character, contributing to our unique perspectives and experiences. So, what happens if the core is weak, damaged, or infected?

Our core beliefs dictate our choices in life. They are somewhat our moral road maps. Core beliefs can be formed due to the values taught in childhood, or they may be altered due to life experiences. Negative experiences can impact a person enough to infect (change) positive core beliefs. Example- (core belief) love is awesome and blissful; there is infidelity in the relationship (infection), and once the infection occurs, a new belief forms - love sucks, and once a cheater, always a cheater. Or the individual may blame self and begin to feel worthless and not enough. Hopefully, this has not happened to you, but if it did, you must act fast.

Negative core beliefs distort your perspective of reality. You believe your truth regardless of how many times it can be proven incorrect. You overgeneralize or have a lack of trust, which perpetuates the negative beliefs. Core beliefs that are impaired interfere with interpersonal relationships. You take the irrational beliefs into your new relationship(s) and eventually lead to damage, constant conflict, toxicity, or termination of the relationship. Untreated infections can kill you and the things connected to you.

Trauma such as sexual abuse, physical abuse, verbal and emotional abuse, domestic violence, codependency, divorce, the loss of a loved one, and other negative life-altering experiences can contribute to a change to your core beliefs. Maladaptive thinking patterns and coping skills are the results of negative core beliefs. The antibiotic to clear up the infection is cognitive restructuring. The Bible states, "So as a man thinketh he is" (Proverbs 23:7). It also states that "Life and death are in the power of the tongue" (Proverbs 18:21). Negative core beliefs are a byproduct of damaged roots.

Peace and love,

Dr. Latoshia

PS. This is getting very personal, my friends, but don't stop. You are working towards your healing. How many licks, bumps, negative experiences, and poor choices will it take to infect your core before you decide to do the work to heal?

Song: "Hope in Front of Me" by Danny Gokey

Go to the Feel-Deal-Heal Journal and complete the writing prompt for LOL #4.

*"What you say can preserve life or destroy it;
so you must accept the consequences of your words."*

-Proverbs 18:21 GNT

LETTER OF LOVE #5: UNCOVER YOUR EQ

Bonjour!

I pray this letter reaches you in good spirits. If this is difficult to manage or the load still feels heavy, keep reading and working. Hopefully, things will begin to turn around.

I have another question for you. Have you ever seen a child carrying around a security blanket? Did you think, "How cute"? I have, and I did. Nowadays, the blankets are fancy with animal heads and all kinds of prints and colors and textile attachments. Why do parents introduce a child to a security blanket?

Security blankets are said to offer emotional support for smaller children in the same way a doll, pacifier, or stuffed animal does. They are said to provide a sense of safety and comfort, especially when the parents are not around or during sleep.

The same thing can happen with emotions. Humans who experience some form of trauma or negative life experiences may develop an emotional security blanket for protection. This may be intentional or unintentional. The aim is to protect yourself from pain or being harmed more. You want to feel safe. You become wary. Your blanket may be anger or aggression. It may be mistrust, envy, bitterness, or unforgiveness. You avoid talking to others so that they can't get close to you. You develop core beliefs matching your behavior to feel justified and safe. I'm sorry to inform you, my friend, that you have given yourself a false sense of security. You have developed a maladaptive way of coping, and it will, if it hasn't already, cause conflict and place a strain on your relationship with yourself and others.

Understanding your emotional responses or reactions will help you develop clear knowledge about yourself and increase your emotional intelligence (EQ). It provides you with more insight on how to respond to others in a positive, compassionate, loving manner when they display negative, rude, or crass behaviors and attitudes. Your goal is to have more self-awareness and self-control to increase positive interactions with others. If you are avoiding or don't understand your emotions and triggers, how can you have compassion, love, and kindness for others? How can you live at peace with others as much as it depends on you-(see Romans 12:18)? It's time to let go of the emotional blanket and increase your EQ score.

Uncover your heart,

Dr. Latoshia

PS. If your emotional security blanket has been handed down from generation to generation, I challenge you to lose the blanket. Give it to Jesus. He knows what to do with it and has better coverage for you.

Song: "Heart on Ice" by Road Wave

Go to the Feel-Deal-Heal Journal and complete the writing prompt for LOL #5.

"Understanding your emotional responses or reactions will help you develop clear knowledge about yourself and increase your emotional intelligence (EQ)."

LETTER OF LOVE #6: DROP THE BAGGAGE

Hello!

I have used the song "Bag Lady" by Erykah Badu in both individual and group therapy. I often laughed at myself as I hummed or sang the song when I was walking from the car to the office. I would have my lunch bag, computer bag, backpack, purse, and sometimes bags with office supplies. The bags kept me from taking the stairs, and they were sometimes difficult to hold while entering the elevator doors. They slowed me down but did not stop me from reaching my destination. Once I got to the office door, I had to drop several of them to open the door.

I know you are wondering why I'm telling you about my physical baggage. As humans, we experience many ups and downs in life. Some encounter more negative and traumatic events than others. Many hold onto the negative emotions attached to the experiences. Some may define their self-worth or who they are due to the events. Holding onto negativity affects your thinking, your self-talk, your behavior, and ultimately your decision. You may feel as though you have moved on from the damaging event, but in reality, you are still carrying it around. Emotional baggage can distort your thinking, impact your decisions, and majorly impair personal and professional relationships.

What are some emotional bags that can weigh you down or crowd your personal space? Good question. The bags can be filled with many things. Life experiences have a way of adding to your already tired arms. Work, family, kids, spouse, etc. Too many hours in the wrong arms fill the bag of shame. Unaddressed offenses and unhealed emotional wounds result in bag after bag of anger, guilt, shame, bitterness, pessimism, anxiety, depression, unforgiveness, intolerance, deceit, impatience, insecurity, jealousy, resentment, low self-esteem, lack of confidence, mistrust, etc., the weight is too much. Baggage places a heavy strain on your relationships - personal and professional.

Some people are addicted to bitterness. They don't want to give up their anger because they believe it shields them from hurt or fuels them. Listen, my friend, if you are carrying around the bag of bitterness or rejection, let it go! It's too heavy. Your back will ache due to the strain. Your heart will remain broken due to the excessive weight. Choosing to remain broken doesn't hurt others; it hurts you and those you love. It increases your fragility. Suppose you continue to hold onto hurtful, painful memories or current negative or stressful circumstances. In that case, you will develop a negative mindset, and then the bags will continue to accumulate, fill up, and weigh you down. Emotional bags get in the way of joy, peace, and happiness. Give your bags to Jesus; He can handle the weight. You must "Cast all your care upon Him, for He cares for you" (1 Peter 5:7).

Drop the load,

Dr. Latoshia

PS. Drop them like they are hot. Let go, and don't pick them back up. Be free. Move forward with your life without all the junkie junk.

Song: "Freedom Chant/ Let Go" by Pastor Mike Jr.

Go to the Feel-Deal-Heal Journal and complete the writing prompt for LOL #6.

*"Give all your worries and cares to God,
For He cares about you."*

-1 Peter 5:7 NLT.

LETTER OF LOVE #7: JERICHO

Greetings!

The last letter was heavy. Did you feel it? I did, and I was more than happy to drop the unnecessary weight. I gave it all to Christ. I hope you did or have made the decision to do so immediately. Make a move towards unloading all unnecessary baggage.

This letter is for those who have gone beyond hauling around baggage to building stone walls. People often build stone walls around their hearts as a protective mechanism. These walls are metaphorical and represent emotional defenses that individuals construct to shield themselves from potential pain, disappointment, or vulnerability. This defensive behavior can be a response to past traumas, heartbreaks, or betrayals. By creating these barriers, people believe they can guard their hearts and prevent further harm. However, while these walls may serve as a sense of security, they also hinder authentic connections and emotional intimacy with others. Breaking down these walls often requires introspection, trust, and a willingness to embrace vulnerability, allowing individuals to experience deeper and more meaningful relationships.

Dealing with difficult situations can cause emotional discomfort and disrupt your daily functioning. One horrible experience can trigger the construction of an emotional wall. Each damaging, traumatic, hurtful, painful, major change, stumbling block or offense can increase the wall's height, length, and thickness. The wall gets thicker whenever you avoid dealing with painful, uncomfortable, and vulnerable situations. The stony wall impacts your personal, professional, and social relationships. You hide behind the wall to avoid personal and intimate connections for fear it could potentially lead to pain, hurt, or rejection. You desire healthy relationships, but your fear and pain are greater than your desire, so you keep the wall up.

My friend, you must allow the wall to come crashing down. It gives you a false sense of protection. Although it may block out the bad, it also prevents the good from entering. The lack of desire to let your guard down contributes to you always being on the defense. When we are always on the defensive, we tend to approach situations with a guarded and suspicious mindset, making it difficult to trust others or to be trusted ourselves. Emotional walls contribute to anxiety, anger, potential paranoia, depression, loneliness, sadness, insecurity, overanalyzing, compartmentalizing, negativity, etc., all are equivalent to Jericho. They block your joy, peace, and happiness.

We get good at protecting ourselves, but at what cost? How long have you been hiding behind your wall? There is nothing behind there that's too hard for God. Trust God to use the hurt, pain, heartbreak, rejection, sorrow, shame, humiliation, depression, and anxiety for good. I encourage you to allow the wall to come crashing down and construct a gate instead. The wall keeps out both the good and the bad. A gate allows you to let out those who do not belong and let in those who do.

God would love for you to give Him everything that keeps you hidden behind your wall. He wants to free you and heal you, but you must be willing to allow the wall to fall. Shame isolates you. Guilt consumes you. Discouragement deters you. Anxiety afflicts you. When you allow the wall to be torn down, you don't lose anything, but you gain protection from the Father. You gain a support system that you can now trust and depend on. Your self-respect, joy, peace, and happiness can be restored. "Be strong and of good courage" (Joshua 1:6). Allow God to have control of your life. Make a loud noise, sound the trumpet, and let your wall come crashing down. You don't have to be afraid.

I understand the wall is comforting. Everyone needs a place where they feel safe and protected when the storms of life hit. God is a shelter. "The Lord is a refuge for the oppressed, a stronghold in times of trouble" (Psalm 9:9). Allow the heavenly Father to build a fence of protection around you.

That way, you can receive those things that contribute to your true peace and happiness and push you toward your purpose.

Sound the trumpet,

Dr. Latoshia

PS. Embrace emotional freedom. Learn to feel-deal-heal

Song: "Break Down These Walls" by Melanie Fiona

Go to the Feel-Deal-Heal Journal and complete the writing prompt for LOL #7.

The LORD is a shelter for the oppressed,
A refuge in times of trouble."

Psalms 9:9 NLT

LETTER OF LOVE #8: EMOTIONAL ROLLERCOASTER

Hello once again,

Did you sound the trumpet and make a loud noise for your wall to come crashing down? If you did, congratulations. If you didn't, it's okay; there is still more work to be done regardless.

Vivian Green has a song where she speaks about being on an emotional rollercoaster due to her romantic relationship. Have you ever taken one of those rides? Unfortunately, I have. I must admit I'm not that fond of amusement park rides. Especially those that go fast and twist up, down, and all around.

Life feels like a rollercoaster at times. Death of a loved one, divorce, loss of income, broken friendships, forbidden relationships, family problems, illness, marriage, graduation, birth, etc. The negative events make the ride daunting and seem to last forever. It begins to slow down and disrupt your daily level of functioning. It throws you off balance and off course. On the ride, you learn how to mask emotions and pretend that all is well. You don't realize that this prolongs the ride. The pretending speeds it back up because things seem to be alright. Then, symptoms related to your reality hit the button to slow the ride down again.

Living with unhealed emotional wounds often resembles riding a rollercoaster, a turbulent journey filled with ups and downs. Just as a rollercoaster climbs and plunges, so do our emotions, swinging from despair to hope, anger to forgiveness, and sadness to joy. To break free from this cycle, it is essential to acknowledge and accept these wounds as a part of your past. By doing so, you take the first step toward gaining control over your emotional roller coaster. Seeking professional support, be it through coaching, therapy, or counseling, can provide guidance and strategies to navigate these tumultuous emotions. Equipped with self-compassion, patience, and a commitment to self-care, you can gradually level the emotional terrain. As you ascend from the depths of unhealed wounds, the rollercoaster may still have dips, but you gain the power to regain control, choose your direction, and ultimately find a smoother, more serene path toward healing and emotional well-being.

My friend, you must deal with your reality (pain, loss, grief, depression, anxiety, fear, etc.) so that the ride will stop and you can get off. It's important to have a strong and healthy support system. It's equally important, if not more, that your support system has a firm relationship with Christ. It's also necessary to learn and apply positive and adaptive coping skills. Don't be afraid to seek professional help by talking to your primary care provider (PCP) or mental health professional (MHP) or get a life coach.

Time to get off the ride,

Dr. Latoshia

PS. My dear friend, some things may be good to you, but they are not good for you. There are things you can and can't control. Learn and know the difference so you can get off and stay off the emotional rollercoaster.

Song: "Emotional Rollercoaster" by Vivian Green

Go to the Feel-Deal-Heal Journal and complete the writing prompt for LOL #8.

"Living with unhealed emotional wounds often resembles riding a rollercoaster, a turbulent journey filled with ups and downs."

LETTER OF LOVE #9:
BREAK FREE

Greetings!

I pray the last letter didn't make you dizzy or sick. A regular rollercoaster ride may be fun, but it can still contribute to an upset stomach or dizziness after the ride. It can also incite fear and anxiety during the ride.

This letter will keep you stationary. When I hear or say the word shackles, I immediately picture a prisoner or someone who is in handcuffs and chains and being held in confinement. Do you see the same image? Have you experienced wearing physical shackles or cuffs? I have, and trust me, they are very uncomfortable and humiliating. Very degrading. In a million years, I would have never guessed that I would be placed in handcuffs and shackles and lose my freedom. My Lord!

You detain yourself mentally and emotionally when you hold onto hurtful, painful, damaging experiences. Unknowingly, you create emotional shackles around your heart and mind that keep you from moving forward. Each offense, negative event or circumstance creates a link to the chain that binds you in a mental prison and eventually stops you. Your incivility, discouragement, uneasiness, misfortune, hostility, aversion, harsh treatment of others, resentfulness, anxiety, depression, and hate all constrain you. Each strong emotion that you hold onto adds a link. Each destructive thought, malicious act, failure to address a situation, or refusal to feel an emotion, tightens the shackles and cuffs. The chains are getting tighter, and you don't recognize it as they are wrapped around your heart and soul. By the time you realize what is happening, you feel emotional paralysis; the chains are cutting off your air supply and distorting your vision. You want to move forward with life, but you can't move, and you can't breathe or see.

Please don't allow sadness, depression, anger, bitterness, shame, guilt, mistrust, unforgiveness, compartmentalizing, and overthinking to paralyze your joy, peace, and happiness. Don't allow them to keep you from being healthy and authentic in your personal, social, and professional relationships. Please don't engage in negative, maladaptive behaviors to cope or numb the pain from the tight chains. Don't allow the shackles to deter you from walking by faith, or the handcuffs prevent you from reaching up and grabbing God's unchanging hand. "Lift your eyes to the hills…your help comes from the Lord…" (Psalm 121:1-2). Once you have Him, you can break the chain by releasing your past and all the pain and secrets connected to it. Don't engage in negative, maladaptive behaviors to cope or numb the pain from the tight chains.

So, what do you do? Good question. Where do you start? That is great question. I'm reminded of an old-school song that stated, "Shackles on my feet won't let me dance. Turn on some music that has a nice beat, and take off the shackles." You must take off the shackles. Okay, you can't identify with that song. What about Tasha Cobbs' "Break Every Chain" or Mary Mary's "Shackles"? The point is that you must remove, break, take off, and get rid of the shackles and chains that have bound you. You do so by identifying and addressing the situations that contributed to the links that formed the chains. Dealing with strong emotions and vulnerable experiences is tough because it makes you uncomfortable. You may have a difficult time expressing your thoughts, emotions, and needs. It's okay! Just start the process; it will become familiar and hopefully easier as you continue. You got this! Let go and let God.

Break every chain,

Dr. Latoshia

PS. It's time to take off those shackles and have liberty **over** **v**ulnerable **e**motions. It's time to cultivate a love mindset, and feel-deal-heal..

Song: "Shackles" by Mary Mary

Go to the Feel-Deal-Heal Journal and complete the writing prompt for LOL #9.

"I look to the hills!
Where will I find help?
It will come from the LORD,
Who created heaven and earth."
-Psalms 121:1-2 CEV.

LETTER OF LOVE #10:
I NEED A GOOD PAIN KILLER

Greetings!

I hope you are free to explore some of the junkie junk we hold onto that contributes to emotional security blankets, damaged roots, emotional bags, emotional roller coaster rides, and your personal Jericho. Oh yeah, and let's not forget those emotional and mental shackles.

Pain, I couldn't think of a clever or witty way to dress it up. Pain is uncomfortable. Pain can be agonizing and to the point of being unbearable. It's multifarious. Pain is unavoidable, and it does not discriminate. You heard me correctly. As long as you are living, at some point, you will experience some form of physical, mental, and emotional pain. I hope that didn't upset you.

The pain we are about to explore requires more than ibuprofen to relieve it. There is a multiplicity of things that can cause physical, mental, or emotional pain. We all suffer pain, but we don't endure it the same. Pain enters our lives at different frequencies and intensities. Some can handle pain or distress better than others. For example, before I say this, don't judge me. LOL. I'm just being honest. I am a big baby when it comes to physical pain. We do not get along at all. I recall the pain from natural childbirth. It was horrible! I didn't think I was going to make it all three times. I'm sure I am in the top 10 for the worst patients during childbirth, lol. The strange thing is that I seem to have a higher tolerance to endure mental and emotional distress. I'm not boasting. In later letters, I will explain this more. I will admit once I realized this about myself, I wasn't sure if it was good, bad, or indifferent.

I'm not sure I can articulate what mental and emotional pain feels like. I do know that individuals who have suffered a harmful or traumatic experience may have difficulty dealing with painful memories. Some may block the memories to avoid dealing with the pain. This prolongs their healing. At some point, the memories will resurface unless you get a traumatic brain injury or some other medical condition that affects memory.

My friend, I want to encourage you to address the pain in your life. Holding onto emotional injuries, past or present, such as unmet expectations, grief and loss, divorce, infidelity, heartbreak, disappointment, misfortune, any form of abuse, rejection, etc., can lead to a mental disorder if you don't address the wounds before they get larger. The pain alters your thinking. You may recall me discussing in previous letters how your thinking affects your speech, and your speech impacts your behavior. Some pain, depending on the severity or how you perceive it, can block your ability to see beyond that moment, nevertheless, to think about living without that which is absent.

If you have suffered one or multiple traumatic experiences, do not allow the pain to keep victimizing you. Don't allow it to define you or your future. You are a survivor now let's be a healed survivor. You are an overcomer. You are awesome. Don't allow your pain to stop you from forward movement. Use your pain to become a change agent in your life and the lives of others. Pain shouldn't be a constant in your life.

Your pain differs from mine, but it does not make either less important. What harms you may not harm me and vice versa, but that doesn't mean we should dismiss one another's pain. It could save a life or two. Christ suffered an agonizing death because He loved us, and He wanted us to be saved. The moral of the statement is that He suffered, He died, but now He lives. Free yourself from the captivity of pain. Turn it over to Jesus. He can handle it.

You are not your pain,

Dr. Latoshia

PS. Depending on the severity or longevity of physical pain, it can contribute to mental distress. Symptoms related to mental distress can manifest in physical pain.

Song: "Survivor" by Destiny's Child

Go to the Feel-Deal-Heal Journal and complete the writing prompt for LOL #10.

"If you have suffered one or multiple traumatic experiences,

do not allow the pain to keep victimizing you.

Don't allow it to define you or your future."

LETTER OF LOVE #11: LOVE IS…

Greetings!

Oh my, are you in the recovery room, or do you still need intensive care to assist you with the infection? Do you need a second opinion? It is my prayer that in the last letter, I was able to help you understand the need to address and heal old and new pain. I need you to stick around. We still have more work to do. Are you ready to get on board the Love Train?

Love, from a biblical perspective, is the greatest commandment and a fundamental and foundational aspect of human existence. 1 Corinthians 13:4-7 beautifully articulates the essence of love: "Love is patient, love is kind. It does not envy, it does not boast, it is not proud. It does not dishonor others, it is not self-seeking, it is not easily angered, and it keeps no record of wrongs. Love does not delight in evil but rejoices with the truth. It always protects, always trusts, always hopes, always preserves." This biblical definition of love highlights the importance of love in nurturing emotional health. Love, when practiced in accordance with these principles, fosters emotional well-being by promoting patience, kindness, forgiveness, and compassion. It enables individuals, such as you and I, to build strong, supportive relationships that serve as a source of comfort and strength in times of difficulty.

The impact of authentic love on emotional health can be profound. In the Bible, it is emphasized that love casts out fear (1 John 4:18), and this rings true in the realm of emotional well-being. When you and I experience love in our lives, whether from family, friends, or a romantic partner, it creates a sense of security and belonging that mitigates feelings of isolation and anxiety. Love provides a safe space for vulnerability, allowing us to express our pain, fears, and anxieties without judgment. It nourishes our sense of belonging and self-worth, filling the voids left by past emotional scars. Authentic love empowers us to let go of resentment, forgive the past, and foster a profound sense of acceptance and understanding. It provides the foundation upon which emotional wounds can mend and transform, fostering resilience, trust, and a newfound capacity for joy and connection. In the presence of authentic love, our emotional rollercoaster begins to stabilize, paving the way for genuine healing and a brighter, more emotionally balanced future.

Love and be loved,

Dr. Latoshia

Song: "Your Love Is" by Calvin Richardson

Go to the Feel-Deal-Heal Journal and complete the writing prompt for LOL #11.

*"Most important of all, continue to show
a deep love for each other, for love, covers a multitude of sins."*

-1 Peter 4:8 NLT

LETTER OF LOVE #12: TAINTED LOVE

Greetings,

I hope this letter finds you well and in good spirits. Today, I want to touch upon a topic that affects us all at some point: tainted love and its profound impact on emotional well-being.

Love, in its purest form, can be a source of immense joy and fulfillment. It connects us on a deep emotional level, nourishing our souls and bringing meaning to our lives. However, love can also be complex and fraught with challenges, especially when it becomes tainted.

Tainted love is like a beautiful painting with hidden cracks beneath the surface. At first, everything seems perfect, and the world is painted in vibrant colors. But as time passes, cracks emerge, revealing a darker underbelly that can lead to emotional turmoil.

Jealousy, possessiveness, and emotional manipulation are common elements that taint love and corrode emotional well-being. These toxic patterns can erode our self-esteem, leaving us feeling unworthy and unlovable. The constant emotional rollercoaster can lead to anxiety, depression, and a sense of helplessness.

The impact of tainted love is far-reaching, affecting the individuals involved and their relationships with friends, family, and the wider community. It can lead to isolation, as the fear of judgment and criticism keeps us from seeking support. We might withdraw from social circles, further exacerbating our emotional struggles.

However, it is essential to recognize that we have the power to break free from the clutches of tainted love. It begins with self-awareness and understanding the signs of a toxic relationship. Setting healthy boundaries becomes crucial in protecting our emotional well-being.

Healing from tainted love involves self-reflection, seeking professional support, and surrounding ourselves with a strong support system of friends and family. By embracing self-love and prioritizing our emotional health, we can embark on a journey of growth and resilience.

Please remember that love should be nurturing, supportive, and uplifting. You and I owe it to ourselves to seek relationships that bring out the best in us, where we can thrive emotionally and feel cherished for who we truly are. Relationships that push us towards our purpose. Those are assets, not liabilities.

Please take a moment to reflect on your own experiences with love and relationships. Let us embark on this journey together, empowering ourselves and those around us to build a future filled with genuine affection, understanding, and emotional well-being.

Cultivate true love,

Dr. Latoshia

PS. Have you heard the phrase "Actions speak louder than words?" This is true for love. There is a difference between professing love and practicing love. For love to grow in a healthy manner, it must be practiced daily. That means being respectful to one another, acknowledging each other, showing affection, and being receptive to it all as well. You should also help one another, spend quality time together, have open and honest communication, and address the good, the bad, and the ugly in a timely and respectful manner. Cultivating healthy love requires you to take responsibility for your actions without blaming. To be always faithful and trustworthy. True love should be cultivated in all relationships – professional, parent-child, romantic, friendships, and family.

Song: "Why I Love You" by Major

Go to the Feel-Deal-Heal Journal and complete the writing prompt for LOL #12.

Love does no harm to a neighbor.

Therefore, love is the fulfillment of the law."

-Romans 13:10 NIV.

LETTER OF LOVE #13: LOVE THY SELF

I hope this letter finds you in good health and high spirits. Today, I want to talk about a powerful and transformative force that can shape our lives for the better: self-love. Embracing self-love can profoundly impact our emotional well-being and healing, leading us toward self-discovery and personal growth.

In a world that often emphasizes external validation and societal expectations, we may overlook the importance of loving ourselves unconditionally. Self-love is not selfish; it is a nurturing foundation that allows us to cultivate a positive relationship with our inner selves. When we embrace self-love, we build a solid emotional core supporting us during life's challenges, helping us navigate difficult times with resilience.

One of the most significant benefits of self-love is its impact on emotional well-being. We develop a strong sense of self-worth and self-compassion when we love ourselves. We learn to accept our imperfections and treat ourselves with kindness and understanding. As a result, we become less affected by external judgment and criticism, and our emotional equilibrium becomes more resilient.

Moreover, self-love is a potent catalyst for healing. When we prioritize our emotional well-being and practice self-compassion, we create a nurturing environment of inner wounds to mend. Embracing self-love allows us to release the weight of past hurts and forgive ourselves for any mistakes we may have made. It enables us to let go of negative patterns and transform into better versions of ourselves.

Self-love is not an overnight accomplishment but a journey that requires patience and practice. It involves identifying and challenging negative self-talk, setting healthy boundaries, and engaging in self-care activities that rejuvenate our mind, body, and soul. Surrounding ourselves with supportive and understanding individuals who encourage our self-love journey can further enrich our emotional well-being and healing process.

In conclusion, self-love is a gift that we can give ourselves unconditionally. Embracing self-love strengthens our emotional well-being, enabling us to handle life's ups and downs with grace and courage.

This internal transformation creates a ripple effect, enhancing our relationships with others and fostering a more compassionate and harmonious world.

I encourage you to embark on your journey of self-love, embracing your uniqueness, and celebrating the beautiful individual you are. May this path of self-discovery and healing lead you to a place of profound contentment and inner peace.

Embrace your truth,

Dr. Latoshia

PS. Self-love is not optional. Your story matters because you matter.

Song: "Love Myself" by Tracee Ellis Ross

Go to the Feel-Deal-Heal Journal and complete the writing prompt for LOL #13.

"*Self-love is not an overnight accomplishment,*
but a journey that requires patience and practice."

LETTER OF LOVE #14: PRICELESS

Greetings!

You made it off the love train. That was an intense ride but prayerfully a helpful journey. Please continue to allow your love for self to evolve into something beautiful and pure, overflowing into the lives of those you love and interact with each day. Let's continue to dig deeper. Yep! There is more to be discovered and uncovered.

When you hear the words invest or investment, what's the first thing that comes to your mind? I'm sure it has to do with finances, in particular stocks and bonds. Usually, when someone makes an investment, they expect to yield a return. Maybe you like to gamble. You take a chance at the slot machine or the Blackjack table in hopes that you will receive back a greater sum than what you put in or down.

Have you ever thought about yourself as an investment? Have you pondered on the things you invest in your relationships with parents, children, siblings, friends, professionals, and romantics? Often, an individual fails to recognize when he/she should let go of a certain relationship. I've been told that some people are in your life only for a season or a particular reason. However, it's unfortunate when you don't realize that a relationship is temporary, so we force something to be what it's not meant to be. You work diligently and desperately to keep the relationship going and healthy. You give and give of yourself and your abilities and amenities. Why?

When you don't invest or believe in yourself, it can make things difficult. Your vision of self becomes distorted. You find yourself lost and not knowing your merit. You settle for less than, or you compromise your values, self, and beliefs. Why? You are afraid to be alone. You sell yourself to the lowest bidder because you fail to recognize that you are priceless. If you don't value yourself and know your worth, then who will? Sometimes, when you love someone, you are willing to change to prove that love. Loving someone shouldn't be at the expense of you devaluing yourself. You shouldn't have to demote or change your values, self-worth, reputation, and morals. I also urge you, my friend, to be aware of the fact that in a relationship (romantic), you should be primary and not the option.

Know thy worth,

Dr. Latoshia

PS. God knows your worth. Christ died because he thought you and I were worth saving. Christ paid a heavy cost to demonstrate how much He loves us. Turn to Him and listen to His will for your life. He will place the appropriate people in your life at the perfect time. Clean out your ears and open your heart, mind, and soul to what He has planned for you. He will receive a return on His investment. Be comfortable enough with who you are so that you don't feel the need to prove yourself to everyone you encounter. Take your running shoes off; you don't have to chase people down or convince them to be in your life. Enhance your self-love by investing in yourself, spending time with you, and believing in you. That's what I have learned to do. Remember, Christ has paid a price for you that no one else can pay. You are too precious to have a man-made price.

Song: "Rain on Me" by Ashanti

Go to the Feel-Deal-Heal Journal and complete the writing prompt for LOL #14.

"Loving someone shouldn't be at the expense of you devaluing yourself."

LETTER OF LOVE #15:
FRAGILE, HANDLE WITH CARE

Greetings!

Wow! It is amazing to know your worth. You are a unique design made by God. That's priceless.

I'm sure you have heard the word vulnerable. You may have been like me and thought it meant some form of weakness; therefore, you avoided it at all costs. What does it mean to be vulnerable, especially with another person? I'm here to help you.

Let's clear the air. Vulnerability doesn't automatically classify you as a "weak person ."It does mean that someone who is in a vulnerable state or position may be an easy target for additional harm because he/she is not at the normal level of functioning. So, you are weak at the moment.

You, I, and everyone else, no matter what race, gender, economic status, or religious belief, need at least one relationship - a connection with someone that allows you to be vulnerable, to rest, and to reset. You must trust someone with your less-than-strong side. You need a moment to remove the cape, take off the mask, and stop pretending long enough to remember that you are a human being. Now listen well. Please make sure that the person you entrust your fragility to - vulnerability to, is someone who will handle you with love and not break you into more pieces.

As a clinician working in a psychiatric hospital for youth and a day treatment school, I had to be trained in a method called Handle with Care. The first part of the training taught me how to de-escalate an upset client verbally. If the situation progressed to where the individual was a threat to self or others, the client was placed in a hold. There were usually at least two people, but I was taught to place the hold alone. When placing the hold, the aim was to keep the client from harm while handling him/her with care - being careful not to cause injury.

There is one person I recommend for the job. You can't see Him nor touch Him, and His voice is not audible. God is truly amazing, and He will handle you with care no matter the situation. He is someone you can be vulnerable with, and He will not tell your business. You can rely on Him and have full confidence in the course of action He tells you to take. He wants to take care of you. 1 Peter 5:6-7 affirms His care for us. "Therefore humble yourselves under the mighty hand of God, that He may exalt you in due time. Casting all your care upon Him, for He cares for you."

God has the ability, power, knowledge, and resources to heal all wounds you may have endured in your quest to love yourself and others. He's a one-stop shop. He has everything you will ever need. He knows what you need more than you. Seek Him. My second warning to you is, before you give your heart away to someone other than God, pay attention to the way those who say they love you protect your best interests. Observe how well they respect you, if they do at all. How do they contribute to building you up and protecting your worth? Do they encourage you to be unapologetically you? Do they take from you and never give to refill you?

Being vulnerable means, as the young people say, keeping it 100. It means being true, raw, and open with yourself about your truths, proclivities, strengths, and weaknesses and then sharing those things with a trusted ally. That can be scary and uncomfortable, especially if you have been burned by people you love and trust. So, you have difficulty letting your guard down and putting in the code for the alarm system. Maybe you have never been given the opportunity to be vulnerable because everyone looks to you to be the "strong one", therefore, you don't know how to be vulnerable.

Lay it all on the line,

Dr. Latoshia

PS. It's difficult to open up when you already have a distorted view of yourself and think that you are damaged goods. However, it's vital to your well-being. Acquire the services of a life coach or therapist until you can safely open up to someone you trust. These individuals are trained and are legally obligated to *ferme la bouche*, close their mouth and can't spread your business.

Song: "Put It All One Me" by Sydney Renae

Go to the Feel-Deal-Heal Journal and complete the writing prompt for LOL #15.

"Pay attention to the way those who say they love you protect your best interests."

LETTER OF LOVE #16:
IT'S A CHOICE

Jambo!

Be honest. How are you feeling? Have the letters been helpful? Have you been doing the work? If so, is it too much, or are you able to handle the content without any problems?

I would like you to focus on an emotion that receives a lot of attention. Anger. When you read the word, what was the first thing that came to your mind? Was it negative or positive? I'm pretty sure it was negative. It is my opinion that anger gets a bad rap. Hold on, I'm about to explain.

Many have asked me if anger is good or bad. So now I'm asking you, do you think anger is good or bad? Ponder on the question as you continue to read this letter. Are you an individual who denies feeling anger for fear others will think you have "anger issues"? The literature on anger is never-ending. Very extensive. Clinician after clinician, researcher after researcher have written books and articles to assist individuals, professionals, etc., with understanding anger and how to maintain control.

In the therapeutic setting, I prompted many clients to draw a tree. In the middle of the tree, I requested the client write the word anger. At the base of the tree, write the words pain and fear to represent roots. Pain and fear are at the root of many people's anger. You may have been hurt by a loved one, someone lied to you, you were raped, and you haven't let go or moved past the pain. You were abandoned as a child, so you fear being left by those you love. You fear others pointing out your flaws, such as the inability to read or you have a lazy eye. So instead of acknowledging your primary emotion, pain, or fear, you decide to feel anger, which is the secondary emotion. Your fear of looking weak, so you save face by expressing some form of aggression to mask. You lack the skill set to deal with the main issues, past or current pain or hurt, etc., so you act out to draw attention from your vulnerable state, failing to realize that anger contributes to vulnerability as well.

Anger is a normal emotion. It's not one we should feel all the time, but you don't have to deny feeling anger nor condemn yourself when you do choose to feel it. Anger can be a natural and involuntary emotional reaction to a perceived threat, frustration, or injustice, but again in many instances it is a secondary emotion because we fail to address the root cause connected to the primary emotions. What would you say if I said anger is a choice? We have a choice in how we feel about varying situations and experiences. If you choose to feel anger due to an uncomfortable moment, it may very well be a valid choice. However, feeling anger is not the issue. It's how you express the emotion. When you hear about someone having "anger problems," it's not anger; it's the individual's behavior that is the problem. Reaction is impulsive. You don't think about your actions. Response is using logic. You make an informed decision. Remember, anger, the emotion, is not the problem; it's the person's behavior that is the major issue, especially if the behavior is frequent.

Let me pause and make this clear. If you suffer from a mental disorder, other factors will need to be addressed as you learn to develop and implement positive and adaptive coping skills to aid in your responding-using logic. You may require professional assistance. It would not hurt to seek help even if you have not been diagnosed with a mental illness. Why? You may need assistance with the identification of root issues and then reframing thoughts and behaviors. For example, you learned to express anger by watching your father. Each time he felt anger, he would hit your mother or say harsh things to you. Now, each time you feel anger, you hit or use harsh language. That's a learned behavior that must be corrected. Your thought process and core belief must be reconstructed. If not, you risk damaging your relationships because of your behavior and not anger, although it may be labeled as an "anger management issue".

So, what does this all mean? When you choose to feel anger, beware of your actions. If you display aggressive or negative behaviors, seek assistance with the identification of the root. You may need to change core beliefs, develop positive and adaptive coping skills, and reframe thoughts related to past negative, uncomfortable, abusive, and traumatic experiences.

Be wise,

Dr. Latoshia

PS. You can choose to respond to your feelings of anger by making a difference. Dr. King was angry about how Black people were being treated. His response was nonviolent, and he continued to show love and build strong relationships. Making a wise choice requires you to be healthy mentally and emotionally. If you have any form of mental impairment or deficit, your ability to make a wise choice will possibly be impaired.

PSS. One last nugget: you must understand the things you can and can't control. Use the diagram in the journal. On the outside heart, identify things you have no control over. On the inside heart, list the things you can control. Hint: if the inside heart includes anything that's not related to you: what you do, what you say, what you believe, what you ponder on, what you value, remove it. That includes your children or spouse if you listed them. Especially the children. You can control the consequences you may give a child if he or she disobeys your directives. The child has a choice to obey or not. If not, then you apply the consequence. You cannot control another human. You can only control how you respond to outside stimuli. Please stop thinking you have control over another human. Please stop trying to gain control. You can also control how often you choose to feel anger. How long do you remain upset, and what is the level of intensity?

Song: "Angry Too" by Lola Blac

Go to the Feel-Deal-Heal Journal and complete the writing prompt for LOL #16.

"Be angry and do not sin;
do not let the sun go down on your anger,
and give no opportunity to the devil."

-Ephesians 4:26-27.

LETTER OF LOVE # 17:
IT'S OKAY NOT TO BE OKAY

Greetings,

I hope you made it through the heat wave alright. Anger's a tricky one, isn't it? But always remember, there are things we can control and things we can't. What matters most is how we choose to respond.

Let's talk about something we often brush aside—loss. Going through one loss after another can really mess with your emotions and impair your mental well-being. It's like each one adds to a pile, making it harder to keep your balance. Processing each loss before the next one hits can feel impossible, leaving you stressed, anxious, and maybe even depressed. Seeking support and coping strategies becomes crucial to keep yourself afloat.

I've been there, between 2017 and 2018, I faced six major losses. At the time, I didn't realize how deeply they were affecting me. Remember when I said I could handle mental pain better than physical? Turns out, it wasn't my strength but God's grace that kept me going. When I strayed from that connection, things got tougher.

Dealing with unaddressed grief is essential for maintaining emotional and mental well-being, as unresolved grief can have profound and lasting effects on your health and happiness. When grief is left unattended, it can fester and manifest in various ways, including depression, anxiety, anger, and even physical ailments. Suppressing emotions related to loss may lead to prolonged suffering, strained relationships, and an inability to fully engage in life. Unresolved grief can also hinder your personal growth and development, as the pain of loss continues to linger beneath the surface, affecting your ability to find meaning and fulfillment. By facing and processing grief in a healthy and supportive manner, you can honor your emotions, cultivate resilience, and gradually find healing and peace.

Please do not rush your healing process, take the time to heal properly. Don't ignore the signs of depression. Acknowledge where you are and seek help if you need it. Don't push away those who care about you. Let them be there for you. Ask them to hush, hug, and hang around. And remember, it's okay not to be okay, but it's not okay to stay that way. Take the time to feel, deal, and heal.

I repeat, seek support from loved ones, counseling, coaching, or spiritual guidance which can provide valuable resources for navigating the complexities of grief and moving forward with renewed strength and clarity.

Open your heart to healing,

Dr. Latoshia

PS. Addressing grief is crucial for preserving mental and emotional stability, as unattended grief can cloud judgment and prompt self-destructive choices.

Song: "Who You Are" by Jessie J

Go to the Feel-Deal-Heal Journal and complete the writing prompt for LOL #17.

"God blesses those who mourn,

for they will be comforted."

-Matthew 5:4 NLT

LETTER OF LOVE #18: RESILIENT HEART

Greetings,

I wanted to continue with grief if that is okay with you. Overcoming grief and healing from the emotional wounds associated with the death of a loved one or any significant loss is a profound and often challenging journey. Grief is a natural response to loss, and there is no set timeline or "right" way to navigate it. Healing typically involves allowing oneself to experience the pain and sadness fully rather than attempting to suppress or rush through these emotions. By acknowledging and processing the grief, individuals gradually find a path toward acceptance and transformation and a new normal.

The series of blows from February 2017 to October 2018 knocked me down numerous times, but I always managed to pick myself back up. Did that make me resilient? Looking back, I realized that while I was getting back on my feet, it didn't necessarily mean I was healing and thriving. The weight of those blows was taking a toll on my mental and emotional well-being. However, my perceived resilience didn't prepare me for the devastating blow that came on April 4, 2019, when I lost my freedom. I turned to God seeking answers: "Why did this happen? Why me?" The questions seemed endless. Seeking solace, I plunged into His Word, unaware that He was preparing me for an even greater loss.

On November 8, 2019, I faced the unimaginable pain of losing my oldest son to suicide. With no family or friends to console me and lacking proper clinical support to help me process everything, I felt utterly alone. The one clinical professional I relied on wasn't accessible when I needed someone to confide in. Our brief time together was marred by the restrictions of being handcuffed, hindering me from feeling secure enough to express my vulnerabilities. However, God graciously provided me with two women who empathized with the anguish of losing a child. They sat by my side, shed tears alongside me, and brought moments of laughter into my life. For their presence and support, I am deeply thankful.

However, God kept me during this time. He gifted me with a peace that I had never felt before. I was able to receive that the things He allowed to happen would be used for good. I no longer sought out the "why" and just began to praise Him and thank Him for what was to come. He assured me that I was not alone and that He had me. God comforted me in my time of grief and loss in a way that brought about healing and understanding of His will and the purpose He has for my life.

My friends, the healing process often includes seeking support from friends, family, or professionals and finding constructive outlets for grief, such as support groups or creative expression. It is essential to remember that healing doesn't mean forgetting; it's about finding a way to cherish the memories and love of those we have lost while continuing to move forward in life and thrive. Over time, the emotional wounds begin to mend, and you learn to embrace your new normal, living with a renewed sense of purpose and understanding of the impermanence of life. Healing from grief is a testament to the resilience of the human spirit and the capacity to find hope and joy even in the wake of profound loss.

Coping with grief and loss is of paramount importance for our emotional and mental well-being. Grief is a natural response to loss, and it is an integral part of the human experience. It is crucial to address and process grief because, unaddressed, it can lead to emotional and mental instability, impacting our relationships, daily functioning, and overall quality of life. Coping with grief provides a pathway to healing, allowing us to find meaning, acceptance, and resilience in the face of loss. It also offers us an opportunity to remember and honor the lives and experiences of those we have lost. By navigating the challenging terrain of grief, we ultimately cultivate emotional strength, and mental stability, learn to cherish the preciousness of life, and find a path toward renewed hope and purpose.

Remember HEARTS coping strategy:

H: Honor Memories – Cherish and honor the memories of your loved one or the source of your loss.

E: Embrace Emotions – Allow yourself to feel a wide range of emotions without judgment or suppression.

A: Accept Support – Lean on your support network, whether it is family, friends, or support groups.

R: Reflect and Remember- Take time to reflect on your feelings and remember the positive moments you shared.

T: Take Care of Yourself – Prioritize self-care, including proper nutrition, exercise, and sleep.

S: Seek Professional Help – Do not hesitate to seek the guidance of a therapist, counselor, or life coach if needed.

Keep healing,

Dr. Latoshia

PS. With God's help, you can rise from the ashes of sorrow and emerge stronger and renewed.

Song: "See You Again" by Wiz Kalifa

Go to the Feel-Deal-Heal Journal and complete the writing prompt for LOL #18.

"It is crucial to address and process grief because unaddressed,

it can lead to emotional and mental instability,
impacting our relationships,

daily functioning, and overall quality of life."

LETTER OF LOVE # 19:
NO FAULT ZONE

Bonjour,

Did the last letter make you uncomfortable? Did you squirm just a little? Some of our junky junk is very uncomfortable. That's why we have been avoiding it. I said our and we because I have been there as well. This next topic may or may not rub you the wrong way.

Jamie Foxx said in one of his songs, "Blame it on the alcohol." Are you that person who waits until you have had one too many drinks and says harsh things to others? Do you blame it on alcohol, or do you blame the actions of others? Or maybe you are sober with your cruel, nasty, aggressive, hurtful, crass, and spiteful behavior. You blame others because of what they did or said or didn't do or say? It's always someone else's fault.

I taught my children at an early age to accept responsibility for their actions, even if it meant getting into trouble. I would not allow them to blame one another when something came up missing or broken. If both were involved, they would have to state their responsibility in the matter. When you take responsibility for your actions and acknowledge your wrongs, you can see how you contribute to your own brokenness, anger, bitterness, petty attitude, etc. You can begin to heal.

Blaming others in the long run only stops you from progressing. It stunts your growth. Exonerate yourself from the heavy load of emotional baggage or break the chains. Also, I urge you to refrain from being a thief. Stop taking the blame for others' actions. You cannot control what someone else says or does. If an individual says something nasty to you because you spoke to him or her, that's not your fault. Please do not blame others for your unfavorable behaviors and feelings, nor take the blame for theirs.

Be honest with yourself. My mother often told my sisters and me that honesty is the best policy. I have also heard the phrase, "Tell the truth and shame the devil. "I never thought about how either one of those statements applies to me being honest with myself. I knew what they meant by engaging with others. As I worked through my own junky junk, I had to acknowledge the need to accept my part in my brokenness. I couldn't keep blaming my parents or past lovers for everything. The acceptance provided me the chance to be truthful with myself and make the necessary changes to avoid traveling down that same road and recollecting the baggage I dispersed along the way.

Did you notice I said dispersed instead of discard? Sometimes, we backtrack to reclaim things that, although hurtful, make us comfortable. The comfort of knowing what to expect from misery. We do the same thing with God. We tell him, Lord, I lay all my burdens at the altar. Take them. However, before you finish your prayer, you start to recollect all your junk, the hurt, anger, bitterness, low self-esteem, blame, shame, daddy issues, mamma problems, and anything that contributes to pain. Free yourself from the chains of blame. Accept the gift of peace from Christ. John 14:27 states, "Peace I leave you with, My peace I give to you that as the world gives do I give to you. Let your heart not be troubled, neither let it be afraid."

Turn it over to the Lord,

Dr. Latoshia

Song: "Blame It on Me" by Akon

Go to the Feel-Deal-Heal Journal and complete the writing prompt for LOL #19.

I am leaving you with a gift –
peace of mind and heart. And the
peace I give is a gift the world
cannot give. So don't be troubled or afraid."
-John 14:27 NLT

LETTER OF LOVE #20: STAY UP

Jambo,

Are you still with me, or are you blaming it on the rain? Just kidding. Hopefully, the last letter assisted you with unloading a lot of weight. The next topic is going to be heavy.

Have you ever been detained or incarcerated physically? Do you know someone who has? Depending on the length of their detention or imprisonment, there are so many individuals who may have lost a sense of what it feels like to be free. Once they receive their freedom, they have difficulty adjusting. They make positive changes. They try to stay on the straight and narrow, doing all the right things to establish their lives. Making parole or probation appointments on time. Staying drug and crime-free. Searching diligently for a job. Yet each probation or parole visit is a reminder of the past. Each rejection from a potential employer or property manager due to their background is a reminder of their past. They did their time, yet they are still being punished. Shame resurfaces. Old wounds are reinjured. In their minds, they are still confined. The ability to readjust is becoming less and less possible. Why? Distress over the guilt of not being successful at obtaining a job or a decent place of their own to stay. The disgrace of going to probation and parole meetings to be reminded of what they did instead of being encouraged to press forward and keep making positive strives.

Maybe you have never been physically incarcerated, but you are mentally imprisoned. Your thoughts detain you. They keep you from being your authentic self. You are too afraid to have the door to your skeletons unlocked. Your shame of past behavior, choices, and mistakes bound you. You are ashamed because you aren't the person you want to be, nor the person everyone thinks you are. You have become a pro at pretending. You always present the fake you. The one everyone believes you are. The distorted thoughts confine you, and you are bound by shame. It will not allow you to be your true self. It reminds you of past mistakes. It keeps the failed relationships on the front-page news in your mind. It constantly reminds you that you are less than, not enough. Shame beats you after each layoff, negative bank balance or bill collector call to remind you of how worthless you are. They tell you that you're dumb, stupid, and unable to maintain anything that's good. Shame tells you that you're incomplete, so you seek out things you thought would make you complete, only for shame to laugh in your face and increase. Now, it adds light to your disfavor. It reminds you of how you compromise your values, worth, and reputation for temporary fulfillment. Shame is very cruel. Each time you try to break free, it appears and tightens the mental cuffs.

Breaking free from mental and emotional bondage is essential for our well-being. When we are trapped in negative thoughts and feelings, it is like being locked away in a 6x8 jail cell. It is vital to remember that shame should never be the warden that keeps us in this dark place. When we allow shame to keep us bound, we deny ourselves the chance to heal and grow. Just as a flower needs sunlight to bloom, we need to release shame to let our spirits flourish. Opening up, seeking help, and showing ourselves compassion and grace are the keys to unlocking the door to freedom. By doing so, we embrace our own humanity and give ourselves permission to embark on a journey toward self-discovery and emotional liberation.

Hold your head up,

Dr. Latoshia

PS. The reason history repeats itself is because instead of allowing it to guide and teach, we fail to learn from it, we allow it to define us, or we ignore it altogether. We must learn to gain knowledge from our poor choices and mistakes. God can use mistakes to promote change for His glory. Allow God to touch the hurting places. He will rebuild you. You must be willing to acknowledge all your faults, repent, and ask for forgiveness.

If we confess our sins, He is faithful and just to forgive us our sins and cleanse us from all unrighteousness, according to 1 John 1:9. Once you ask Him for forgiveness, it's done. You must also forgive yourself. One of the strategies that the devil uses against the believer is the reluctance or inability to forgive self. I will go into more detail about forgiveness later. For now, as the young people say, stay up. Don't allow shame to bring you down.

PSS. Mistakes are made once or twice, but the repetition of the same behavior is an intentional choice.

Song: "Keep Ya Head Up" by Tupac

Go to the Feel-Deal-Heal Journal and complete the writing prompt for LOL #20.

"Mistakes are made once or twice,
but the repetition of the same behavior is an intentional choice."

LETTER OF LOVE # 21: DON'T HIDE BUT SEEK

Hello friend,

Didn't I tell you that the last letter would be some heavy stuff? I don't know about you, but I am glad to be rid of all that junk. With all this weight coming off, I may consider running a marathon. Sike! That is an entirely different mental challenge that I have yet to master; nonetheless, the physical aspects of running a marathon. I digress. Well, it's my prayer that you are still staying up. This next topic may cause you to duck. Remember, we are getting rid of your junkie junk, so hold your head up.

Escape has a song that states, "You're my little secret, and that's how we should keep it." I know it's old. Let me make my point, please, and thank you. Little secrets over time become larger secrets, which lead to secrets being exposed. My mother used to tell my sisters and me that what's done in the dark will come to light. I learned my first major lesson with this when I became pregnant in my 12th-grade year. If she didn't know I was having sex, she was about to find out without a doubt.

Not only the exposure to my mother, but I didn't know how I would handle the coach. So, I decided to hide it. My goal was to finish the season without him knowing. We were halfway through the season, and I talked to key people: my boyfriend, my mother, and my doctor. All agreed with my decision to keep playing. However, somehow, a rumor started going around the school that I was pregnant. Coach asked me about it, and I denied it. The second time he confronted me which was a few weeks later, right before a game. He called me and one other senior to the locker room. He stated, Daniels, I keep hearing that you are pregnant. I gave in. The funny thing is that I never admitted to him that the rumor was true. I politely got up and left the meeting location without confirming or denying it. I went to the female locker room and placed on my clothes. My high school basketball days were over. I left the coach standing, waiting for a verbal answer. I walked out and never gave him an answer.

The act of keeping secrets can have a profound impact on one's mental and emotional health. Secrets can weigh heavily on the mind, causing stress, anxiety, and even depression. When we hide important information or conceal our true thoughts and feelings, we create a cognitive burden that consumes mental energy. This constant internal conflict between what is known and what is hidden can lead to a state of heightened stress, as the fear of the secret being discovered, or the guilt associated with keeping it eats away at your peace of mind. Over time, this chronic stress can contribute to a range of mental health issues, including increased levels of anxiety and emotional instability.

From a biblical perspective, the dangers of keeping secrets are underscored by the idea that truth and transparency are integral to a life of righteousness and moral integrity. In Proverbs 28:13, it is written, "Whoever conceals their sins does not prosper, but the one who confesses and renounces them finds mercy." This verse highlights the perils of secrecy, suggesting that hiding one's transgressions or maintaining deceitful secrets can lead to spiritual and moral decay. Secrets can fester within the heart, eroding one's character and distancing them from a righteous path. I got a testimony for that.

My friends, the act of keeping secrets carries profound implications across the realms of mental, emotional, and spiritual well-being. Mentally, the burden of secrecy can lead to heightened stress and anxiety as the secret holder grapples with the constant cognitive dissonance between their hidden truths and the external world. This inner turmoil can erode mental clarity, hinder concentration, and even contribute to symptoms of depression. Emotionally, secrets can be a breeding ground for a range of negative emotions, including guilt, shame, and fear. The emotional toll of hiding one's true self or concealing significant information can fracture self-esteem, trigger emotional instability, and strain relationships, leading to feelings of isolation and loneliness. From a spiritual perspective, secrets can create a disconnect between the person holding a secret and their values or beliefs, as the act of hiding truths may conflict with principles of honesty and authenticity. This spiritual misalignment can lead to a sense of inner turmoil, potentially impeding personal growth and the pursuit of more profound, authentic spiritual connections. Thus, the implications of keeping secrets are intricate and interconnected, impacting not only the mind and heart but also the soul's journey toward fulfillment and enlightenment.

Come out of hiding,

Dr. Latoshia

P.S. Your secret is not safe from the God who sits high and looks low.

Song: "Confessions-Part 2" by Usher

Go to the Feel-Deal-Heal Journal and complete the writing prompt for LOL #21.

*"People who conceal their sins will not prosper,
but if they confess and turn from them,
they will receive mercy."*

-Proverbs 28:13 NLT

LETTER OF LOVE #22: TAKING OWNERSHIP

Greetings!

Are you still hiding, or have you begun to seek forgiveness from those seeds of deception that ruin you? Do you know the Bible tells us not to lie to one another? Seriously, "Don't lie to each other…"-Colossians 3:9. Read it! It has some other helpful pointers for putting on your new nature and learning how to exemplify the characteristics of our Creator. Honesty is still the best policy. Think it…Speak it…Do it…think the truth, speak the truth, walk in the truth, face it, love it, and pursue it. Let honesty become your new energy. Habit energy creates habit self; what you do often becomes a habit, and that habit becomes you.

Not only should you be honest with others, but you should be honest with yourself. Have you ever felt off-balanced or that something wasn't right with you, but you couldn't pinpoint the problem, nevertheless, the source? Have you ever recognized that things weren't "normal" in your life? Family and friends keep mentioning to you that "something is different about you." They may ask, "What's wrong with you?" They seek to understand the change, yet you lack an answer.

Taking ownership of our emotional well-being is a necessary act of self-empowerment and self-care. It requires intentionality and commitment to understanding our emotions, acknowledging their validity, and taking proactive steps to heal and grow. This process often involves introspection, seeking coaching, therapy or support when needed, and learning healthy coping mechanisms. By taking responsibility for our emotional state, we reclaim control over our lives, fostering resilience and self-compassion.

Healing can be a challenging journey, but it is a testament to our strength and determination to live a fulfilling, restored life. We are able to be more than just survivors; we are healed survivors who thrive.

Assuming ownership of our thoughts, speech, and behavior is a pivotal step in nurturing our overall emotional well-being. Our thoughts influence our emotions, and our words and actions affect both ourselves and those around us. By recognizing the power we hold in shaping our internal and external worlds, we can make intentional choices to foster positivity, empathy, and personal growth. This involves self-awareness, questioning negative thought patterns, promoting constructive self-talk, and aligning our actions with our values. When we actively engage in this process, we become architects of our emotional health, constructing a life enriched with mindfulness, empathy, emotional health, and resilience.

Get your life,

Dr. Latoshia

PS. "A man's pride will bring him low, but the humble in spirit will return honor" (Proverbs 29:23). Don't allow pride to keep you from self-care. You do a disservice to yourself, those who love you, and those who interact with you. "Let your speech always be with grace, seasoned with salt, that you may know how you ought to answer each other" (Colossians 4:6). It's on you to respond to others in a warm, gentle, and honest manner. Stop blaming others for your harsh words. "Keep your tongue from evil, and your lips from speaking deceit (Psalm 34:13). Remember, "A soft answer turns away wrath, but a harsh word stirs up anger" (Proverbs 15:1). Take ownership of your junkie junk and gain and maintain self-control. "Regulate your mind; get yourself together." The mind is a battlefield, but God can see you through. He's a mind regulator.

Song: "Help" by Erica Campbell feat. Lacrae

Go to the Feel-Deal-Heal Journal and complete the writing prompt for LOL #22.

"*Assuming ownership of our thoughts, speech, and behavior is a pivotal step in nurturing our overall emotional well-being.*"

LETTER OF LOVE#23: COUNT UP THE COST

Greetings!

Did the last LOL motivate you to get your life? It is a common tendency among some individuals to avoid taking responsibility for their troubles. Instead of acknowledging their role in the challenges they face, they may engage in blame-shifting or denial. This reluctance to accept responsibility can hinder personal growth and development, as it prevents individuals from learning from their mistakes and making positive changes in their lives. It is important, my friends, to remember that taking responsibility for one's actions and circumstances is a crucial step toward finding solutions, seeking help when needed, and ultimately moving forward with a sense of empowerment and accountability.

Before I continue, I want to acknowledge that if some of my letters seem to be repeating themselves, your thoughts are correct. Repetition is a fundamental element in both learning and unlearning processes. When we are acquiring new knowledge or skills, repeated exposure and practice help solidify and reinforce what we have learned. In contrast, when we are trying to unlearn old habits, beliefs, or behaviors, repetition is essential for breaking down established neural pathways and replacing them with new, desired ones. It serves as a means of reprogramming our minds and reshaping our perspectives. Repetition allows us to gradually let go of the familiar and embrace the unfamiliar, making it a powerful tool for personal growth and transformation. Whether we are striving to acquire fresh insights or rid ourselves of detrimental patterns, the consistent repetition of new information or behaviors is the key to achieving lasting change.

This next subject can be very costly if you refuse to take heed and do the work. Forgiveness is a profound and liberating act that offers healing to the forgiver. When we fail to forgive others for their offenses, we carry the heavy burden of resentment, anger, and bitterness within us. These negative emotions can corrode our well-being, erode our peace of mind, and even harm our physical health. The cost of holding onto unforgiveness extends beyond us, affecting our relationships and perpetuating cycles of hurt and conflict. In contrast, forgiveness brings a sense of freedom and inner peace, allowing us to move forward with a lighter heart and a healthier spirit. It opens the door to reconciliation, restoration, and the opportunity for both parties to experience growth and transformation. Ultimately, forgiveness is a gift we give ourselves, as it frees us from the chains of the past and enables us to embrace a brighter, more compassionate future.

The devil often exploits unforgiveness as a powerful tool to keep us ensnared in a cycle of bitterness and distraction, pulling us away from our spiritual path and God's intended blessings. When we harbor unforgiveness, we become consumed by resentment, vengeance, anger, and negative emotions, diverting our focus from the things of God and weakening our connection with Him. This separation from God not only hinders our spiritual growth but also obstructs the flow of His abundant provisions and blessings in our lives. Unforgiveness becomes a stumbling block on our journey of faith, preventing us from experiencing the fullness of God's grace, love, and purpose. To break free from the devil's grip, it is essential to heed the call to forgive, allowing God's transformative power to restore our relationships, heal our hearts, and renew our spiritual vitality.

Can you afford it,

Dr. Latoshia

PS. "For if you forgive other people when they sin against you, your heavenly Father will also forgive you. But if you do not forgive others their sins, your Father will not forgive your sins"
– Matthew 6:14-15 (NIV).

Song: "I Forgive Me" by James Fortune

"I Forgive You" by Nicole Norton

Go to the Feel-Deal-Heal Journal and complete the writing prompt for LOL #23.

*"Forgiveness is a profound and liberating
act that offers healing to the forgiver."*

LETTER OF LOVE #24: THE STRUGGLE IS REAL

Greetings!

Has unforgiveness broken the bank? It is my prayer that if it has, it will be repaired, and those things you lost, you can get an upgrade when and if they are given back to you. Watch your thoughts, speech, and actions. You don't want to say or do anything that will cause you to lose something you can't afford to be without. You can't afford to be without Christ.

Have you ever failed a test? You may be thinking, how many? It's discouraging. I had a female client who was in the 11th grade at the time. She was excited about taking her driver's test, but she needed to study. I got a driver's manual for her and several other teen clients. A week or so later, everyone claimed to be prepared to take the written portion of the test. All of them went at various times over the course of about two weeks. The first week, two passed, and one failed. The one who failed in the first week went back the following week and walked away successfully.

My female client went the second week, and she failed. We processed her thoughts and feelings. We reviewed her study habits; I quizzed her, and she made some adjustments in her study process. She failed a second time. I sought to find a solution to her failure. I questioned the two who passed the first time. Both stated they used the telephone and let the lady read them the questions. I asked the third guy what he did differently the second time to pass. He also stated that he used the phone option. He received advice from the first two, and he utilized it. I took the advice and passed it along to my female client. She said "Okay," but test after test, she failed. From the time I gave her the advice until the time she successfully completed the test, she had taken it 12 times. I would ask her each time if she used the phone option. Her response would be, "I don't need it."

So, what was the problem? She was too prideful to use the accommodation to assist her with passing the test. The others recognized their area of weakness and accepted the help that was available. Their acceptance led to victory.

Do you resonate with the experience of my teenage female client? Life throws a challenge your way, and there are people who've been through the same thing and can help. Support and accommodations are at your disposal to ensure you success. Yet, you choose to forge ahead independently. Perhaps thoughts like "I'm no fool," "I've got this handled," or "I can figure it our on my own" dominate your mindset. There's a conviction that assistance is superfluous. Recognize that these thoughts are detrimental, misleading, and ultimately restricting your potential for growth and healing.

Choosing to take heed to help rather than letting pride hinder us is a courageous act of wisdom and humility. Pride often blinds us to our limitations and prevents us from seeking assistance when needed. However, recognizing that we cannot do everything alone and acknowledging our vulnerability can lead to growth and positive change. By humbly accepting help, we open ourselves to the collective wisdom, experience, and support of others. It is a testament to our strength of character when we prioritize progress and teamwork over the need to appear self-sufficient. In doing so, we not only overcome challenges more effectively but also strengthen our relationships, fostering a sense of unity and camaraderie within our communities. Accepting help is a powerful testament to our commitment to personal growth and our willingness to extend grace to ourselves and others.

Don't be stubborn,

Dr. Latoshia

Song: "No Pride" by Kieran the Light

Go to the Feel-Deal-Heal Journal and complete the writing prompt for LOL #24.

"Pride leads to disgrace,
But with humility comes wisdom."

-Proverbs 11:2 NLT

LETTER OF LOVE #25: BREAKING POINT

Greetings!

Accepting that the struggle can be real is the first step towards meaningful change. Life's challenges, while daunting, become more manageable when we make the conscious decision to take heed to help and ease the burden. It is a courageous acknowledgment that we do not have to navigate the difficulties alone.

Have you ever thrown up your hands in the middle of a task out of frustration? In that moment, did you verbalize failure by stating, "I give up"? Have you ever felt that way about your life? Have the problems in your life felt overwhelming, intolerable, intimidating, and unstoppable? You cried out, wondering when it would end.

Throwing your hands up in frustration is a common response when faced with life's relentless challenges. However, adopting the same mentality towards life's woes and enduring them without pause can throw us off balance, leading to emotional and mental exhaustion. Over time, this unrelenting burden can contribute to diminished mental capacity, making it harder to think clearly, solve problems, and maintain a positive outlook. It is crucial to recognize that it is okay to seek support and take breaks when life becomes overwhelming. Just as we need rest to recharge our physical bodies, we also need moments of respite to preserve our mental and emotional well-being. In acknowledging our limits and practicing self-care, we can better equip ourselves to navigate life's challenges and maintain our mental clarity and resilience.

Reaching your breaking point can be a severely challenging and transformative experience. It is the moment when the accumulated stress, pressure, or adversity becomes overwhelming, and you feel like you can no longer carry the weight of it all. While it may feel like a breaking down, it can also be seen as a breaking open. This juncture can serve as a catalyst for self-discovery and growth. It is an opportunity to reassess priorities, seek support, and make necessary changes to protect your mental and emotional well-being in these moments of vulnerability; you may find the strength to rebuild and emerge even stronger, armed with a deeper understanding of your limits and increased resilience to face life's challenges with renewed vigor and wisdom. Reaching your breaking point is not a sign of weakness but a call to listen to your inner self and take action to restore balance and good health.

Keep your balance,

Dr. Latoshia

P.S. Don't allow an inundation of problems to cause you to break and stay broken. Ask God for help. He can make the pain go away. Don't allow your problems to keep you bent over let God loose you.

Song: "Make Room" by Jonathan McReynolds

"Just Want You" by Travis Greene

Go to the Feel-Deal-Heal Journal and complete the writing prompt for LOL #25.

"Don't allow an inundation of problems to cause you to break and stay broken."

LETTER OF LOVE # 26: SURVIVAL SKILLS

Greetings!

Let's continue to focus on your healing. I must help you get off the injury reserve list so you can do more than just exist. It is time for you to be more than a survivor. It's time to be a healed survivor. Someone who can move forward with life and not just live but THRIVE!

Have you ever gone to the dentist due to pain? You were told that to relieve the pain, a tooth extraction was necessary. You are instructed not to worry because you will be numb as they take the tooth by force. So, you relax. The area is numb, and before you know it, the tooth is out. However, several hours later, when the numbness begins to wear off, you feel the pain, but it is worse than what you felt before the procedure. You take a pain reliever to ease the tension. The pain subsides each time you take medication for relief.

Many people find themselves struggling to heal from emotional injuries, often resorting to various methods to alleviate the pain associated with their emotional wounds. These methods include but are not limited to things such as alcohol, drugs, food, sex, gambling, excessive shopping, staying busy, affairs, and poor relationships, etc. These maladaptive coping methods can provide temporary relief, but they often lead to long-term consequences. Instead of addressing the root causes of their emotional pain, individuals using these coping mechanisms find themselves trapped in a cycle that perpetuates their suffering. It is crucial to understand that these behaviors may offer short-term escape, but they hinder the healing process, erode mental and physical health, strain relationships, and prevent genuine emotional growth. Recognizing the impact of maladaptive coping methods is the first step toward seeking healthier alternatives that promote true healing and well-being.

When it gets to a point where you can't resist or frequently engage in maladaptive behaviors, then it becomes an addiction. When we lose our capacity for enduring discomfort, we lose hope, and joy, and our light is dim or doesn't shine at all. Maladaptive or destructive coping methods are like placing a Band-Aid on a busted head and expecting it to mend on its own. It can also be a covering that prevents a wound from healing. It is time to uncover the wound and feel-deal-heal.

Regain Feeling,

Dr. Latoshia

P.S. It's easy to lose faith and turn to other methods to cover, block, or numb emotional discomfort. You must cease using relationships as crutches, illegal drugs, excessive drinking, etc., to avoid dealing with previous or current injuries. The use of destructive coping methods only adds insult to injury. It is time to turn to the Source who has the resources to assist you with your healing process. God's grace is more than sufficient for addressing your open wounds and scars. FYI, it's okay to have Jesus and a therapist.

Song: "God is Changing Your Story" by Jekalyn Carr

Go to the Feel-Deal-Heal Journal and complete the writing prompt for LOL #26.

"*It is time to uncover the wound and feel-deal-heal.'*

LETTER OF LOVE #27: NOT YET

Greetings!

I hope you are still with me. Did you need to change some or all of your survival skills? If you need to make changes, do it ASAP. Your life is at hand.

Have you ever been driving, and it began to rain so hard you couldn't see the road? The inability to see impairs your progression forward. If you continue blindly, you are putting your life in danger. Have you ever gotten so upset and discouraged about your life? Your problems aggravated old wounds from the past that you decided to end it all? You make the attempt, but you are unsuccessful. You try again and have another failed attempt. You are still alive. Do you know why? Because God said, "Not yet."

Satan does not attack his own. He tries to kill God's children. When you give him access to your mind, he will do everything in his power to kill, steal, and destroy you. Especially if he has been allowed to peek into your future and he realizes just how much of a threat you are to him. So, he tries to use you as a tool to your own demise. The reason you weren't successful with completing suicide is that God stepped in and said, "Not yet." He still has work for you to do. You have not fulfilled the purpose He's attached to your life. "Being confident of this very thing, that He who has begun a good work in you will complete it until the day of Jesus Christ" (Philippians 1:6).

You do not have to hold your head down in shame because of your past actions. If you allow shame to settle, you are giving satan a digital key to access your mind. Accept that you are human. Realize and acknowledge that all have made poor choices at some point and will continue. It's okay not to be okay. However, don't lose sight of the fact that trouble doesn't always last. Suicide is a permanent solution to a temporary problem.

Hold on! Change is coming. There is no need for you to go into survival mode and try to fix things for yourself and alone. Get over your spiritual amnesia and reflect on those things God has already brought you through. Do you recall the miracles He has already performed for you? God knows your troubles, and He can fix any situation if you allow Him. You must turn to Him in your time of trouble. "God is our refuge and strength, a present help in trouble" – Psalm 46:1. You must allow Him to protect you, even if that means from your own self. God can and will bring you out of every and any situation, no matter how major or minor. He promised to be with you as you go through, "When you pass through the waters, I will be with you; and through the rivers, they shall not overflow you. When you walk through the fire, you shall not be burned, nor shall the flame scorch you" – Isaiah 43:2 (NKJV). No problem you face is too big for God. Don't lose sight of who you are and what God can do. "Cast all your care upon Him, for He cares for you" – 1 Peter 5:7.

U Matter,

Dr. Latoshia

PS. You are special, and your life matters. You matter. Your troubles will end, and God is near to see you through if you allow Him. He knows exactly what you need to not only survive but be healed and thrive. Don't allow pain to distort your vision and cause you to give up. Remember, U MATTER.

Song: "I'll Find You" by Lacrae

Go to the Feel-Deal-Heal Journal and complete the writing prompt for LOL #27.

*"So do not fear, for I am with you;
do not be dismayed, for I am your
God. I will strengthen you and help
you; I will uphold you with my
righteous right hand."*

-Isaiah 41:10 NIV

LETTER OF LOVE # 28: STICKS AND STONES

Hello!

There's a song that states, "It ain't over until God says it's over." No matter what you may face, ending your life is not the solution. Turn it over to God. He can heal all wounds. Allow the Lord to fix the damaged places of your past. If your pain and discomfort are current, allow Him to address your current distress. You matter!

As a child, I remember hearing peers make the statement, "Sticks and stones may break my bones, but words will never hurt me," which has long been presented as a mantra to promote resilience in the face of verbal insults. However, it is a myth, for words for words indeed hold the potential to inflict deep, severe emotional wounds. Unlike physical injuries, the pain caused by hurtful words often lingers, impacting self-esteem and mental well-being. The emotional scars from hurtful language can persist far longer than the memory of physical injury. This recognition underscores the need to acknowledge the significance of the impact of words and to prioritize kindness and empathy in our interactions, as they have the power to both heal and harm, sometimes far more than sticks and stones.

Acknowledging the pain caused by harmful words is a pivotal aspect of emotional healing. Denying or trivializing the impact of hurtful language can perpetuate the cycle of emotional suffering. When individuals and society as a whole recognize the deep wounds that words can inflict, it opens the door to genuine empathy, compassion, and support for those who have been hurt. By understanding the emotional injuries and its lasting effects, we can promote an environment where individuals feel safe to express their feelings and seek help when needed. This acknowledgment serves as the first step in the process of healing, allowing individuals to confront and address the pain, find resilience, and ultimately rebuild their self-esteem and emotional well-being. It reinforces the notion that words have the power to both harm and heal, emphasizing the importance of choosing them carefully and responsibly in our interactions.

Hurtful words have a deep and lasting impact on one's mental and emotional well-being. They have the power to wound deeply, leaving emotional scars that can persist long after the words are spoken. Such words can erode self-esteem, trigger anxiety and depression, and create a sense of worthlessness. I was teased as a child and teen. I did not recognize the impact of those hurtful words until I began to unpack emotional baggage. The emotional pain caused by hurtful words can affect how we show up each day and how we interact in our personal relationships, leading to mistrust and withdrawal or people-pleasing. It is essential to recognize that the wounds inflicted by hurtful words can linger, shaping our self-perception and influencing our interactions with others.

Healing from emotional injuries caused by harmful words is paramount for our overall well-being and the harmony of society. The scars left by verbal wounds can affect a person's self-esteem, mental health, and relationships. Unaddressed emotional injuries can lead to a cycle of pain and perpetuate negative thought patterns. Furthermore, in a broader context, an accumulation of emotional injuries can result in a culture of resentment and hostility, hindering productive dialogue and collaboration within communities. By prioritizing the healing process, we not only help ourselves regain our self-worth and inner peace but also contribute to the cultivation of a more compassionate and empathetic society where respectful communication and emotional well-being are valued. Emotional intelligence becomes an acquired knowledge to obtain. Where hurt people no longer hurt people. In doing so, we recognize the enduring impact of words and the need to mend the damage they can cause.

"Death and life are in the power of the tongue; and they that love it shall eat the fruit thereof" – Proverbs 18:21 (ASV). Be intentional about speaking the Truth to replace the lies.

Drop the dead weight,

Dr. Latoshia

P.S. "Do not take to heart everything people say" – Ecclesiastics 7:21 (NKJV). Remember QTIP – quit taking it personally. When hurtful things are said to you, acknowledge your emotions, deal with the situation, and heal.

<table>
<tr><td>Song: "Speak Life" by TobyMac</td></tr>
<tr><td>"I Speak Life" by Donald Lawrence</td></tr>
</table>

Go to the Feel-Deal-Heal Journal and complete the writing prompt for LOL #28.

> *"Some people make cutting remarks,*
> *But the words of the wise bring healing."*
>
> -Proverbs 12:18 NLT.

LETTER OF LOVE #29: JUST AS I AM

Jambo!

Do you feel lighter? Have you begun to heal from the pain due to damaging words? It is my prayer that healing is taking place. I encourage you to become a healed survivor who thrives.

This letter will demonstrate my ability to be authentic and vulnerable. Each time I let down my guard in a letter, I feel lighter, accomplished, and free. Unloading unnecessary weight is awesome. I am glad I can share with you and assist you in your healing process as well.

I enjoy music. To listen to it, dance to it, or sing it. Music gets me, and I get music. The problem I have is I can't tell you eight times out of ten who sings the song. Sad, I know, but it's my truth. Now, if it is my favorite artist, then I got you to a certain degree, LOL.

Kelly Price has a song that ministered to me at a time in my life when I lost perspective of who I was. I didn't know my importance, my value, or my worth. I often felt as though I wasn't good enough. "Just As I Am" reminds me of God's love and acceptance.

In the song, she talks about struggling with self-esteem and the inability to know her importance. On her journey to self-discovery, she recognized that there was nothing wrong with her. She acknowledges God's hands created her, so, therefore, she's exactly who God created her to be. I love the lines, "Lord, you made me just how you wanted me to be. Sharpened in the image of you." To know your value and significance based on what God has put in you is knowledge worthy of obtaining.

Have you struggled with knowing who you are or the ability to define your worth? I know that women speak of this struggle more than men, but I also know that some men have this struggle as well. Events such as divorce, rejection, tragedy, adultery, and trauma trigger strong emotions that lead to thoughts of shame, guilt, insecurity, and more. Distorted thoughts contribute to low self-esteem, lack of confidence, lack of self-love, self-compassion, self-acceptance, and unforgiveness of self. A lack of knowledge of self may contribute to you being more defensive, impulsive, or indecisive.

There's a poem by Frank Outlaw that states, "Watch your thoughts, they become words. Watch your words, they become actions. Watch your actions, they become habits. Watch your habits; they become your character. Watch your character, for it becomes your destiny." Negative thinking leads to negative speech, which contributes to negative behaviors. Thinking negatively about yourself leads to you speaking death into your life. "Death and life are in the power of the tongue, and those who love it will eat its fruit" – Proverbs 18:21 (NKJV). Speak life into your mind, body, and soul.

Celebrate who you are,

Dr. Latoshia

P.S. It is important for you to know thyself and know your worth. Your attitude and choices are a direct result of your perspective, or lack thereof, of yourself. Don't allow difficult and painful situations and people to define you. Remember you are "fearfully and wonderfully made" – Psalm 139:14. God didn't mess up when He made you. If you thought He did, as I did, you were the one in the wrong, as I was as well. Work on learning about yourself so that you will know your worth. If you believe in yourself as much as God believes in you, then you will walk in a confidence that will cause your haters to hate even more. So, from now on, tell yourself, "By the grace of God, I am what I am" – 1 Corinthians 15:10a (NKJV). You are the visual image of God

Song: "Just As I am" by Kelly Price

"Just As I Am" – Deitrick Haddon

Go to the Feel-Deal-Heal Journal and complete the writing prompt for LOL #29.

"Don't allow difficult and painful situations and people to define you."

LETTER OF LOVE #30: STILL STANDING

Greetings!

Is there a celebration going on in your honor? Did you identify your God-given uniqueness and thank God for specialization? You are worth celebrating. Embrace every inch of your being. I dare you to fall in love with yourself. I double, no triple dare you.

Have you ever tried to protect others from going through a storm with you? Have you pretended to be okay just so they wouldn't worry about you? Have you held loved ones at arm's length to keep them from seeing wounds and scars from past storms? You push away your loved ones because although you really need them, you are afraid for them to see the superglue that's barely holding you together. You fear they will discover your truth. They will locate the closest full of masks that you use to pretend that you got it together and can handle what life's throwing at you. They can't know that damage control is still necessary from the last storm. You need the Red Cross First Responders, but instead, you cover up and move swiftly and carefully so as not to show any signs of injury or pain.

As difficult as it may be to trust, you must give people, especially those who love and care about you, a chance to be there for you the way you have been there for them. When you are fragile, you need love more than ever. Don't try to recover alone and risk struggling emotionally without support. Don't push others away or tell lies to make your family and friends think you are stronger than you really are so they can leave you alone and not worry.

I am guilty of pretending to be okay to keep everyone from worrying about me. In hindsight, it was a terrible choice. My masonic brother Karl would call me to see how I was doing. I found myself sounding like a broken record. I would tell him, "I'm still standing," to quickly get him to change the subject. I didn't want him worrying about me. I didn't want him, or anyone for that matter, to know my inner life was in total chaos. I had a few individuals, including my brother, who knew bits and pieces, but not the truth, the whole truth, so help me God. Shame would not allow me to open the door all the way. Just enough to where everyone could see that I was still standing.

There were days of not being motivated enough to get out of bed. I was down, hopeless, and was carrying around too much weight. Most days, I would force myself to get up. Once I was standing, I went into autopilot and pretending just became natural to the point where I began to believe I was good. I would look at the problems with this mindset: the bills are behind, but I'm standing. There is enough food for the kids to eat, but not me, but I'm standing. Through each trial and tribulation, I would repeat the phrase. I was standing but barely. Honestly, I was just existing because my life was in disarray from every angle.

I often felt like a hypocrite. Here I was, this person of influence who could reach down and help others up and assist them with not only standing but walking forward, and some began to run. I would often wonder why it was so difficult for me to help myself. It wasn't until the aftermath of my last major storm that the answer was revealed to me. I held others to a higher degree than myself. Their lives were more important than mine. This was not an intentional thought pattern or words that I verbalized, but it was clear through my actions. I was helping others live without any hesitation, and I was slowly heading to my demise. Friends, I encourage you to get the help you need. Please let it be by choice and not by force. Never allow pride to keep you from the opportunity to be vulnerable with those who know and love you and receive help.

It's your turn to be helped,

Dr. Latoshia

Song: "Need Someone" by Mary J Blige

Go to the Feel-Deal-Heal Journal and complete the writing prompt for LOL #30.

"*Never become so prideful that you miss the opportunity to be vulnerable with those who know and love you and receive the necessary help.*"

LETTER OF LOVE #31: LET IT SHINE

Greetings!

How are you doing? I know I have challenged you to dig deep. I pray you are still standing but with less weight on your shoulders. This next subject will not cause you to use a lot of mental energy.

Have you heard the phrase "natural born talent"? Have you heard someone reference an athlete as one who is a "natural-born athlete?" Both phrases simply mean that the individual does not have to work hard at certain things. They have a natural ability to complete tasks or skills with ease. It just comes easy for the individual. Now, just because one was not born a natural athlete does not mean the person cannot train to become an outstanding athlete. If I recall correctly, Michael Jordan, my all-time favorite, was not immediately identified as a star. He had to work hard for it.

Just like natural-born athletes, there are some individuals who can recover or adjust easily after disruptions of life occur. These individuals are referred to as having resiliency. Just like the athletic example, resilience comes naturally for some, and others work to perfect the skill.

The ability to overcome and bounce back from adversity easily is a gift worth having. So, if it doesn't come naturally, how does one obtain resilience? I'm glad you asked. To cultivate resiliency:

1. Acknowledge and accept the situation for what it is at that moment. Develop a positive and growth-oriented mindset, where setbacks are viewed as opportunities for learning and personal development.

2. Identify the things you can and can't control. Those things you do not have any control over, let them be. Identify if you have a problem that can be solved or a predicament that you must learn to cope with. If it's a problem, (**S**)top and (**T**)hink about what you will do or say and the consequences. (**A**)cknowledge your feelings and (**R**)espond to your problem; use the STAR method.

3. Practice self-care, maintain a healthy lifestyle, and manage stress effectively are essential components of resilience.

4. Setting achievable goals, staying adaptable and teachable, and developing effective problem-solving skills.

5. Develop and implement positive and adaptive coping skills.

Each one of these things helps with navigating adversity more effectively.

Lastly, you must learn how to apply God's Word to your life. Learn to find peace during the suffering. Learn to depend solely on God's direction and His provision for all that you need. Increase your faith, and DO NOT doubt. Focus on the promises of our Heavenly Father. Use your weapons of spiritual warfare, Scripture, songs of praise and hymns, prayer, and worship. Remind yourself that pain equals progression. Pain can propel you to your purpose. Become familiar with the understanding of James 1:1-6 and Romans 5:1-5 and stand firm on Deuteronomy 31:6.

Get your shine on,

Dr. Latoshia

P.S. No matter if you are naturally resilient or if you must cultivate it, make sure your light continues to shine. The Bible says, "Let your light so shine before men, that they may see your good works and glorify your Father in heaven"- Matthew 5:16. So, sing it loud and sing it proud, "This little light of mine, I'm going to let it shine."

PSS. Glow up so others can see how God shows up.

Song: "Show Jesus" by Jamie Grace

"Talkin Bout (Love)" by Maverick City Music feat. Kirk Franklin

Go to the Feel-Deal-Heal Journal and complete the writing prompt for LOL #31.

"Pain can propel you to your purpose."

LETTER OF LOVE #32: LEAN ON ME

Greetings!

Are you shining bright like a diamond? Please don't allow people and problems or predicaments to dim or shut off your light. One way to ensure your light remains bright is to get or maintain a strong support system.

My mother has three daughters, and I am the oldest. She calls us her "three angels". Being the oldest, I took my job as a big sister seriously. I did everything I could to protect my sisters and to care for them when they were left in my care. As an adult, I continue to take my position seriously. So serious that in a trying season of my life, I failed to realize that my little sisters were grown women whom I could have leaned on for support.

Many of my friends would call me if they needed unbiased advice, a listening ear, and support. I love helping others. If someone was in distress, I would drop everything to aid them in any way. There are times I would be on "E," yet if someone needed me, I did my best to get to them or hold the phone, lending my ear to do my best to give them some cheer or to dry their tears.

I must confess. I am pretty good at being a helper. I am not so good at being helped. I would not ask for help because of shame and fear. The two would tag team me and inform me that a helper can't be weak. I would feel guilty when I needed assistance. I felt like a failure. I would push people away. If I did share my distress, it was only surface stuff that those close to me could detect regardless.

The importance of having a support system and trusting it cannot be overstated. Allowing your support system to help you, even when you are usually the one providing support to others, is crucial for maintaining your own well-being. It is a reminder that seeking assistance is not a sign of weakness but an affirmation of your humanity. Just as you extend care and compassion to others, you deserve the same kindness from those who care about you. By allowing your support system to lend a helping hand, you not only receive valuable assistance in times of need but also reinforce the bonds of trust and reciprocity within your relationships. This willingness to accept help when necessary, ensures that your support system remains strong and sustainable, and it affirms that you too, are deserving of love, care, and support from those who cherish you.

Stop being stingy,

Dr. Latoshia

PS: We all need somebody to rely on for support. The song states, Lean on me when you're not strong. I'll be your friend. I'll help you carry on." My current predicament has afforded me the opportunity, by force, to receive help and support from family, friends, and strangers. Ecclesiastes 4:9-12 tells us that two are better than one. So, when you fall, there is someone there to help you up. If you are in danger, there is someone there to help you fight. God's Word also says, "Bear one another's burdens, and so fulfill the law of Christ"-Galatians 6:2. In the past due to my lack of esteem, I failed to see when the Scriptures also applied to me. That it was okay for me to get help as well. The sad part about it is, in hindsight, it was revealed to me just how many individuals I had who were responsible enough that I should've shared ALL my weaknesses and pain, and they would've continued to love me, support me, and hold my hands as I healed. When satan has access to your mind, he will manipulate you to where you become blind, and you can't see all the tools you have for healing. You must deny his access, revoke his security clearance, and have nothing to do with his lies and deception.

Song: "Lean on Me" by Kirk Franklin
"Lean on Me" by Bill Withers

Go to the Feel-Deal-Heal Journal and complete the writing prompt for LOL #32.

*"Share each other's burdens,
and in this way obey the
law of Christ"*

-Galatians 6:2 NLT.

LETTER OF LOVE #33: SHAKE THE HATERS OFF

Greetings!

Who are you leaning on? Whomever you choose, please make sure the person is trustworthy. Everyone can't handle or appreciate your story. Make sure the individual or individuals are pushing you towards your purpose.

Anyone who knows me or who has had a few encounters with me knows I am not a fan of social media. I call it "the devil". Now, I know social media has some positive aspects, but unfortunately, people use it more for evil than they do for good. It is amazing how quickly someone will share someone else's misfortune, spread rumors or provide self-righteous, judgmental comments about another person's situation. With social media, it can be shared in a matter of seconds. You trip and fall, and no one is stingy. You earn your doctoral degree, and those same individuals who were quick to share your fall suddenly forget how to share. To celebrate someone's suffering is sickening. However, I have learned that haters love to hate.

In LOL# 28: Sticks and Stones, we discussed how words can hurt. Our aim is to not allow those who harm with words to win. Don't allow the words and actions of haters to cause you to hold your head down, become depressed, or feel less than others, and please don't take their words personally.

If the words or actions of haters bother you and contribute to your emotional distress, please listen to the word of God. "If the world hates you, you know that it hated Me before it hated you. If you were of the world, the world would love its own. Yet because you are not of the world, therefore, the world hates you"-John 15:18-19. Now, if Jesus had haters, you know you will as well. Now, the Father expects a certain behavior from His children regarding haters. Off top, you may not like it, but obedience is better than sacrifice. So, "Love your enemies, do good to those who hate you, bless those who curse you, and pray for those who spitefully use you"- Luke 6:27-28. Not only are you to love them but feed them if they are hungry and give them something to drink if they are thirsty. Your obedience will lead to Him preparing a table before you in the presence of your enemies.

Now, if you are a hater, you too should take heed to God's word. John 8:7 states, "He who is without sin among you, let him throw the first stone." Luke 6:37 states, "Judge not, and you shall not be judged. Condemn not, and you shall not be condemned." My mother would play a song, The Williams Brothers "Sweep Around." It stated, "Sweep around your own front door before you try to sweep around mine." The group was letting the haters know about Matthew 7:3-5, "Hypocrite! First, remove the plank from your own eye, and then you will see clearly how to remove the speck from your brother's eye." So, you may want to worry about your flaws, problems, secrets, etc., instead of sharing the business of others. Mind your business. "You reap whatever you sow"- Galatians 5:7.

Shake 'em off,

Dr. Latoshia

PS. "Let no corrupt word proceed out of your mouth, but what is good for necessary edification, that it may impart grace to the hearers" – Ephesians 4:29. If you don't have anything nice to say, that includes sharing negative or hurtful posts, then don't say it or share it. "Do unto others as you would have them do to you" – Luke 6:31. If you fall, get back up. If your haters laugh or talk about you, do as the song says, "Shake them haters off." All have sinned and fall short of the glory of God" – Romans 3:23

Song: "Motivation"(clean) by T.I.

"Shake Dem Haters Off" (clean) by Quint Black

Go to the Feel-Deal-Heal Journal and complete the writing prompt for LOL #33.

"Love your enemy,
bless the one who curses you,
do something wonderful for the one who hates you,
and respond to the very one who persecute you
by praying for them."

Matthew 5:44 TPT

LETTER OF LOVE # 34: WHAT ABOUT YOUR FRIENDS

Greetings,

Are you still shaking off your haters? Shake them off and then use them to elevate you to the next level. Shaking off haters is crucial for maintaining emotional well-being and self-confidence. Haters are hell-sent. I encourage you to now allow their negative words and actions to define you, impair your self-perspective, or deter you from your path. By focusing on your growth, inner strength, and God's Word, you can move forward with resilience and self-assuredness, regardless of the difficult and unlovely people you encounter.

During my healing journey, I became more familiar with how emotions affect relationships. I began to ponder about my relationships with friends – those from childhood and adulthood.

True friendship is a precious gift that enriches our lives in profound ways. It provides a sanctuary where we can be our authentic selves, free from judgment or pretense. The impact of true friendship goes beyond companionship; it offers unwavering support, empathy, and a sense of belonging. In times of joy, friends celebrate with us, amplifying our happiness, and in moments of sorrow, they stand by our side, providing solace and understanding. True friends inspire us to grow, to be better versions of ourselves, and to face life's challenges with courage. They are the anchors in the storms of life, the ones who remind us that we are not alone. The significance of true friendship lies not only in the joy it brings but, in the resilience, and strength it imparts, making life's journey all the more meaningful and fulfilling.

During my GAP (God Allowed Pause) season, I learned the valuable lesson of knowing who sent a person into my life. Just as God will send the right people to aid us and push us toward our purpose, satan also will send people. He will use them as tools to kill, steal, or destroy something in our lives, to distract us from what God has called or is calling us to do. Therefore, we must be careful about who we call friends and who we associate with. They come disguised as God-sent, but they are hell-sent. Unhealthy associations can drain our emotional energy, erode our self-esteem, and hinder our personal and spiritual development. Recognizing the signs of toxicity, such as constant negativity, disrespect, or manipulation, is the first step toward making a change. Letting go of that which is sent to kill you.

God has always placed people in my life at the right time. It just took me a while to learn the lesson that everyone is not sent by Him. Some are hell-sent. In my GAP season, He has revealed to me my true friends and their obedience to Him by displaying the true values of a friend in Ecclesiastes 4:9-12 and Galatians 6:2. I can be honest and say that who I believed would be in my corner in hardship is not present. But God…He has sent the right people, and I am grateful.

If you want to identify your true friends, go through a major storm. Many will stick around in a minor storm, but the storm that's off the scales will show you who truly loves and supports you. Your ride or die will be revealed. I am blessed to say I have several "ride or die" friends. I no longer call them friends but sisters.

At the time of writing this letter, I sat in a cold jail cell. My sister-friends have been holding me up as they fight to make sense of my situation. They were with me during the minor storms, but I failed to see their true value. I guess because I lacked seeing my own.

You can count on me,

Dr. Latoshia

PS. "As iron sharpens iron, so a man sharpens the countenance of his friend" – Proverbs 27:17. Genuine friends do not care about why you have fallen as much as they want to know how you are doing and how they can help lift and hold you up. They stand with you through the remainder of the storm and through the recovery process. They don't leave you to heal alone.

PSS. I also have a friend in Jesus. He knows the worst about me, yet He still loves me. He sees the best in me. He does not use my imperfections to humiliate me, manipulate me, or harm me. He does not hold my past or mistakes, mishaps, and misfortunes against me. He values me. He is a friend to me even when I am not friendly to myself. He is forgiving, and His love is unconditional. I encourage you to accept Jesus as your friend.

Song: "What About Your Friends" by TLC

Go to the Feel-Deal-Heal Journal and complete the writing prompt for LOL #34.

"Genuine friends do not care about why you have fallen as much as they want to know how you are doing and how they can help lift and hold you up."

LETTER OF LOVE #35: NEW OUTLOOK

Bonjour!

Do you have loyal friends? Are you a true friend? Can you all count on one another through thick and thin? It is my prayer that you will get or maintain true friendships, but more importantly, know who is God-sent and who is hell-sent. You will be able to avoid a lot of heartache and pain.

Have you ever been too stubborn to change your view on something? Have events, struggles, problems, and experiences contributed to you having a different outlook on life? For some individuals, they can use problems as a motivator to seek solutions and increase knowledge and wisdom. For others, the struggles of life can contribute to a negative perspective on life.

James 1:2-3 states, "My brethren count it all joy when you fall into various trials, knowing that the testing of your faith produces patience." When problems enter your life, you don't have to be happy about the situation, but you should have a positive outlook. Why? Because of the results that trials can produce. Patience is a by-product of faith being tested. Problems can teach important life lessons, grow you, and move you closer to your divine destiny.

James 1:4 states, "But let patience have its perfect work, that you may be perfect and complete, lacking nothing." God is the Potter of your life. He shapes you into the person He needs you to be to fulfill the divine plan He has for your life. He has placed a divine purpose in you. While you are waiting for Him to calm or end your storm, He is working on and in you. He will restore you. You will come out refined, complete, and whole. Have you ever sought after something, a relationship, thinking it would make you special and whole? God is the only one who can complete you. He will give you what you need to be whole. Change your outlook when troubles come. He is working on you to give you the wholeness that you seek.

The importance of adopting a new perspective in the process of healing from emotional wounds cannot be overstated. Often, our emotional scars are linked to rigid patterns of thinking and perceiving the world around us. A fresh perspective can offer us the chance to view our experiences from different angles, providing insights and understanding that were previously masked. It allows us to reframe our past and present in a way that empowers us rather than holding us captive to pain. Through a new perspective, we can shift the weight of guilt, blame, and negative self-judgment, making room for self-compassion, grace, resilience, and personal growth. It is a powerful tool in the journey of emotional healing, offering a path to liberation from the shackles of our past and the opportunity to embrace a more hopeful and fulfilling future.

It's how you look at it,

Dr. Latoshia

PS. Trials are tools God uses to get your undivided attention.

Song: "Better Days" by Le'Andria Johnson

Go to the Feel-Deal-Heal Journal and complete the writing prompt for LOL #35.

"So we don't look at the troubles we can see now; rather, we fix our gaze on things that cannot be seen.

For the things we see now will soon be gone, but the things we cannot see will last forever"

-2Corinthians 4:18 NLT.

LOVE NOTE #36: GROWTH SPURT

Greetings!

I hope things are going well. Have you begun to make necessary changes to view your life from the lens of love – God's perspective? A love perspective prepares you for your purpose as you deal with your problems.

My middle son complained of knee pain when he was in middle school. I took him to the doctor, and we were informed that he was growing faster than the ligaments were forming in his knees. Therefore, the pain was due to bone touching bone. He was in pain because he was going through a growth spurt.

Just like physical growth spurts, you can have a spiritual growth spurt. What is a spiritual growth spurt? I am glad you asked. Before I answer your question, let me provide you with some background as to how the answer was revealed to me.

On April 4, 2019, a raucous storm invaded my life. I was caught off guard, so I did not have time to prepare or take cover. After the storm was over, I began to assess the damage that was done and the impact it would have on my life moving forward. I determined that it was too much damage and to consider a total loss. From the treatment I received from others and the crass and uncouth comments that were made, I believed recovery would not be possible. During the assessment, I failed to recognize that I had an assurance policy and that I could file a claim. That full recovery was not only possible but necessary.

I began to pose many questions to God. I needed answers. I needed to know why. Why me? Why this? Why now? Why my life? Lord, why to this magnitude? Why so much damage? Why such exposure? It did not make sense. I began to search His Word for answers. I read the Old Testament and took notes on how various individuals dealt with and overcame harsh circumstances and life-threatening struggles. I still was not satisfied. The whys remained. So, I read the New Testament. I studied parable after parable. I studied the life of Jesus because I needed answers. Then, I began to read Romans. Chapter five called out to me. The first five verses spoke loudly to me. The funny thing is that not even a year prior, my pastor had walked us through the Book of Romans. I studied the chapter with my life group. This time, a deeper understanding was revealed. This time, a major calamity was trying to claim my life, and the damage appeared as though it would do just that.

The first verse reminded me that we are justified by faith; without faith, we have nothing. The verse showed me that faith brings about peace and joy. God declared us not guilty through Christ so that we can draw closer to Him. I needed more, so I kept reading. I was desperate to gain knowledge and understanding. The pain was too much. "And not only that, but we also glory in tribulations, knowing that tribulations produce perseverance; and perseverance, character; and character, hope"- Romans 5:3-4. I was like, "Hold on, Father. In this disaster, are You telling me to find the strength to praise and worship You? Did You not just see the mass destruction and devastation that ripped through my life? My life is changed forever because of it, and in the aftermath, it is trying to claim my life."

After several weeks of sifting through the wreckage, studying, and praying for understanding, I began to get my questions answered. As I write this letter, I continue to wait for answers. However, I was taught through my studies that suffering or problems are a part of life. We must gain an understanding that tribulations grow us if we stop complaining long enough to learn the lesson. Hardships and attacks from the enemy can be used to build character under the care of the Lord. It is not so much about the trial as it is about how you behave during the trial. We rejoice in suffering not because we enjoy pain or deny its tragedy but because we know God is using our struggle to refine us, to clean us up, to repolish us. He also strengthens us during every trial. The ultimate goal is to trust the LORD in the storms because He has overcome the world.

The next time you face trials and tribulations, look at them as growing pains and look forward to your growth spurt. God is maturing you. God can turn any situation around, and glory is due to Him. "All things work for the good to those who love God and who are called according to His will"- Romans 8:28. You must grow and be developed because He has "Plans for you…plans to prosper you and not to harm you, plans to give you a future and a hope"- Jeremiah 29:11.

It's time to grow up,

Dr. Latoshia

PS. Before God can bring you to your destiny, He must make sure you can handle the responsibility. So, as you go through the test, be confident in the fact that the Lord is going to bring you out victoriously. He is still in the blessing business, and He can still perform miracles. Have faith that He will do it for you. There is a purpose behind your pain. Allow God to salvage your life. Begin your journey to feel-deal-heal.

PSS. Tribulations are essential for true character development.

Song: "8:28" by Lacrae

Go to the Feel-Deal-Heal Journal and complete the writing prompt for LOL #36.

*"In the same way that gold and silver
are refined by fire, the Lord
purifies your heart by the tests and trials of life."*

-Proverbs 17:3 TPT

LETTER OF LOVE #37: NO PAIN, NO GAIN

Hello,

How are you doing? Are you growing? Are you healing and dropping unnecessary weight? God is simply amazing. He can use pain to grow us. Wow! If you think that's something, then the next subject will blow you away.

Have you tried to workout either alone or with a group or a personal trainer? Did you hear the phrase, "No pain, no gain," thrown at you as a motivator? Did it motivate you or frustrate you?

As an athlete who played many sports, I would always push myself to be better. I wanted to be one of the best, if not the best. That meant bearing the pain. I had to pay the price if I wanted to win the prize. Pushing my body to limits it was not used to. I still use the phrase to prompt myself to complete one more set of burpees or to finish the last ten jumping jakes to reach 300. The goal is a lean, toned body and healthy heart and lungs. It will not occur without pushing my body beyond its normal limits. The consequence is pain, but the reward is Tina Turner's legs and Angela Bassett's arms when she played Tina. (Smile).

I know you are wondering what this has to do with emotional disturbance, or Jesus, for that matter. Just like the gain you acquire after enduring the physical pain of working out, the same can occur in your spiritual life. If you are living at some point, you will face adversity. When you sustain injury due to a broken heart, divorce, loss of a loved one, losing your job, losing your home, spouse being abusive, or past trauma from childhood or past relationships, you carry the pain. Some know how to deal with the wounds to heal appropriately, and others continue to hold onto the pain. You may even wonder why God is allowing so much pain and strife in your life. Don't worry; I posed the same question to Him. I wanted to know why He allows us to suffer.

Are you ready for the answer? Well, you already know you can grow from pain. It can also prepare you for birth. However, God sometimes allows tribulation to get your attention. He is trying to get you ready for delivery, but you have your attention elsewhere. He is trying to get you in place to birth your purpose. Due to your focus being on something or someone else, He sends or allows hardship to get your attention.

The pain of childbirth, while intense and challenging, serves a clear purpose – it brings forth new life. Similarly, the pain of unhealed emotional wounds is a sign that something within us needs mending. Just as the pain of childbirth is a passage to a new beginning, the pain of emotional wounds guides us toward personal growth and transformation. These pains, though different in nature, remind us of the precious cycle of renewal, where healing and a new beginning are possible for those who seek them with an open heart. No pain, no gain.

Get ready to push,

Dr. Latoshia

PS. Your pain has a purpose.

Song: "Greater Is Coming" by Jekelyn Carr

Go to the Feel-Deal-Heal Journal and complete the writing prompt for LOL #37.

"Count it all joy when you fall into various trials, knowing the testing of your faith produces patience. But let patience have its perfect work, that you may be perfect and complete, lacking nothing."
— James 1:2-4 NKJV.

LETTER OF LOVE # 38: TAKE OFF THE MASK

Greetings!

Are you still with me? The pain is worth the gain, but you must have faith and allow God to guide you through it. He is a mind regulator, a doctor in the sick room, an attorney in the courtroom, and He will be your midwife when you are ready to birth your purpose. God is truly amazing. Hold on; you aren't ready for the final push because you must rid yourself of a few more things.

I teased a friend about me seeking employment as an exotic dancer to help generate extra income so I could stop borrowing from Peter to pay Paul and then borrowing from Paul to pay Peter. Remember, don't judge. Anyway, I told her my name would be Mystery, and I would wear a mask to keep my identity a secret. Although I was teasing regarding the job, sadly, the mask was already a part of my daily attire. I would not recognize it until after the major storm.

Have you ever felt the need to hide your truth out of shame and fear? Do you fear rejection or abandonment by family and friends, lovers, etc., if you reveal the person hiding underneath the mask? False persona. The person you are trying to avoid showing due to your past has a story worth telling. Experiences, good, bad, pretty, or ugly, serve as the Potter's wheel, shaping the clay of our souls into vessels of unique purpose. Each joy and sorrow, triumph and tribulation, is a chisel carving the intricate design of our character. Through these trials, we are molded, transformed, and refined. When we wear the masks of shame and guilt, we conceal our true selves from the world. These masks, though seemingly protective, carry a burden that distorts our authentic essence. They cast shadows on our self-worth and hinder the clarity of our purpose. To remove them and be free is to embrace the light of self-acceptance and the wisdom that comes from vulnerability. In our ability to embrace our experiences, both joyful and painful, we can find the path to self-discovery and a deeper connection with others, liberated from the weight of shame and guilt.

I encourage you to remove the masks that keep you from being completely honest with yourself and your loved ones about your needs, your struggles, and your pain. Shame and guilt can birth isolation, self-doubt, worthlessness, lack of confidence, the feeling of not being enough, and more. Each broken promise, lie, affair, heartbreak, rejection, disappointment, or loss is hurtful and can contribute to you deciding to keep hiding behind shame, fear, or denial. Each cover you put on to protect your truth can set in motion symptoms related to depression, anxiety, addiction, rage, blame, resentment, and unexplained grief. Delusional thinking. You embrace a false identity, a false sense of self. It is time to take off the mask(s) and feel-deal-heal.

Peek-a-boo, I see you,

Dr. Latoshia

PS. You must be honest with yourself and others. Take off the multiple masks and stop pretending. Aren't you tired? If you are not okay, speak up. Ask for help. Please stop covering up. You are beautiful. You are also human, which means you are not perfect, so there is no need to be ashamed or fearful of being your genuine, authentic self. Everyone has a past with some flawed, regrettable moments. If you are hiding because you fear exclusion, there is no need to fear. Jesus loves you and will always include you. He loves you without the mask.

Let go of trying to be everything to everyone. Identify who you are and how you want to live your life. Each day, make a choice to show up and be your beautiful, authentic self. In the words of an old Kodak commercial, "Let your true colors shine through. "Be honest with yourself and let go of the facades. Extend grace to yourself. You will have more time to spend with yourself and others. Pretending takes up too much time and energy.

All the colors (experiences) in your life tell your story. Don't be ashamed of or feel guilty about your truth.

Song: "Shame" by Summer Walker

"The Real Me" by Natalie Grant

Go to the Feel-Deal-Heal Journal and complete the writing prompt for LOL #38.

"All the colors (experiences) in your life tell your story.

Don't be ashamed of or feel guilty about your truth."

LETTER OF LOVE #39: NO DOUBT

Bonjour!

Do you feel free now that the mask is gone? Look in the mirror and see the masterpiece God created. Own your truth; it is what makes you, you. That which can be changed to enhance a better you, change it, but only for you. Keep your natural beauty. FYI, beauty comes from within. The outer appearance will fade, wrinkle, etc., over time.

"No matter what I face. No matter what may come. I am confident in this God's got me." Lyrics from a song I lack knowledge of the title or singer. Yes, I still have that one problem, lol. However, I did look up the information, "God's Got Me" by Dexter Walker & Zion Movement featuring Minister Time White. This song makes a bold statement of faith. It is an unwavering faith. It is talking about trusting God in all circumstances - present and future. It is a confirmation that God is always with you and I. Wow!

Do you have that kind of confidence? Having a God-confidence during tough times means putting your trust in the belief that God is with you, even when life gets really ugly and hard. It is like having a sturdy support in the stormy seas. This confidence gives you and me strength and courage, helping us face challenges and difficulties with the knowledge that we are not alone. It is a reassuring feeling that no matter what, there is a higher purpose and a guiding hand to help us through the darkest times. With God-confidence, we find the inner strength to weather the storms and come out stronger on the other side. It also provides us with peace that surpasses all understanding as we press forward.

During life's hardships and the healing of emotional wounds, we trust in God as an anchor for our souls. With unwavering faith, we confidently lean on His divine ability to both protect and guide us. Just as a lighthouse stands firm amidst raging seas, God's presence illuminates our path in times of turmoil. As we traverse the difficult terrain of healing, this trust in His guiding hand provides solace and direction. We find that His protection is not just a shield from external forces but also a balm for the inner turmoil of emotional wounds. It is in this unwavering trust that we gather the strength to weather the toughest of times and embark on the journey of healing, knowing that we are not alone but cradled in the loving embrace of His providence.

Doubting God during the hardships and healing casts a shadow on our faith and resilience. Such doubt can be like a heavy barrier preventing us from moving forward in our journey. It can erode the hope that sustains us, making it difficult to find solace and purpose amid trials. In moments of doubt, we may lose sight of the divine plan, and our healing process can be hindered. It is in these times that the reassurance of faith becomes a beacon, guiding us through the darkest hours and offering the strength needed to heal and endure. Doubt, while natural, reminds us of the importance of nurturing our faith as we navigate the challenges of life, for in faith, we often find the resilience to overcome even the most shattering storms. We walk by faith, not by sight. We must have faith in sight to remove the shadow of doubt.

Stand steadfast in your faith and remember no matter what you have done, God will forgive you. No matter the severity of the pain you have suffered, God can heal you. He will stand with you as you go through the test. He will be with you in the recovery room. Faith in God is necessary. If you don't have it, get it. His power is mightier than anyone or anything in your life. When the devil tries to attack you, pray. When problems come one after the other, read God's Word and pray. When your thoughts become distorted and overwhelming and cloud your vision, put some Word on it. Then pray, read, praise, and pray some more. Seek spiritual and professional guidance as well. God placed people on this earth who can help you. Please understand that God has all power, but you can limit

Him with your doubting. In His time, He will restore and resurrect you. If He did it for Lazarus, who was physically dead for four days, do you really think He can't or won't handle your issues? Let go and let God have His way. God's got you!

Stop with the uncertainty,

Dr. Latoshia

PS. Faith the size of a mustard seed is all you need. Let it be unmovable

Song: "I Got That (Remix)" by Anthony Brown & Group Therapy

Go to the Feel-Deal-Heal Journal and complete the writing prompt for LOL #39.

"Trust in the LORD with all your heart,
And lean not on your own understanding."

-Proverbs 3:5 NKJV.

LETTER OF LOVE #40: EXODUS

Greetings,

How are you feeling? Have you decided to place your ALL in the hands of the Father? Trust me, He can handle it. There is no reason to doubt the Creator of heaven and earth. He is our Great Physician and can heal your brokenness and pain if you give it ALL to Him.

On April 4, 2019, I was knocked down by a massive storm. I was blindsided with no time to take cover. The life that I built for my children, and I changed in the blink of an eye. Once the wind calmed, the rain ceased, and I was able to see again the mass destruction was too much to bear. I didn't think recovery efforts were possible. To revive that which was left of my life did not appear to be an option. I wanted to die. Little did I know I was about to die. Not a physical death but a spiritual one. If I didn't die, it would also place my natural life in the wrong hands. I had to die so that God could revive me.

The beginning of the process was not easy. I lacked motivation due to being in shock, confused, and afraid. Nothing made sense to me. I needed answers, but the person who could answer was silent. I was at a loss with little to no hope. My family came to visit faithfully. They made sure I could call them each day. They gave me words of encouragement and told me how much they loved me, needed me, and believed in me. They assured me that they would stand by me through the recovery process. They did not judge me. Their main concern was for my well-being.

Little did any of us know the healing and recovery process was going to begin immediately. Being alone with my thoughts was very difficult. I was told to focus on myself, but I didn't know how. I quickly found out what to do. All I had was Jesus and no one or nothing else. I did not have a Bible for several weeks, so I had to rely on my memorization of the Scriptures. I prayed, quoted Scripture from memory, and sang every song that came to mind, old and new. I did not fight what was happening. Mainly because I was ignorant of what was occurring. Instead of fighting against myself and allowing negative thoughts to consume me, I trusted God. I recognized the need to fight for my life. I was trying to fight for my natural life. I had yet to recognize that, at the moment, the spiritual life was the focal point.

"Dying to self" involves surrendering my will and desires to align with God's will, way, and Word. I recall being led to Galatians 2:20, where Paul states, "I have been crucified with Christ; it is no longer I who live, but Christ lives in me; and the life which I now live in the flesh I live by faith in the Son of God, who loved me and gave Himself for me" – (NKJV). I committed this verse to memory. I made an intentional choice to let go of my way of thinking, my desires, selfish ambitions, and worldly attachments and instead sought to live in accordance with God's teachings and values. I chose not to allow my current predicament or positioning to define me or contribute to my pulling further away from God. Instead, I gave my life back to Him and leaned in real close.

Once God revealed to me which life I was fighting for, I began to give Him everything. The dying process is not easy, nor does it feel good. It reveals the good, the bad, and the ugly about the real you. Things you may have forgotten. A revelation of things you didn't realize about yourself, things you were in denial about, and the things you avoided due to suppression. Looking in the mirror without a mask is not easy. Especially when you have worn the mask for so long that you believe it was your natural appearance. Surrendering your whole heart, mind, body, and soul to Christ is not an easy task as well. However, it is necessary and worth the pain that you endure throughout the process.

One of the lessons I have learned that I would like to share with you is about self-labeling. I had to quickly learn to rebuke this mindset so that it would not hinder my healing journey. This is the act of defining or identifying yourself based on circumstances, predicaments, mishaps, mistakes, roles, positioning, and conditions. It involves adopting labels or descriptions that may be limiting or negative, such as saying, "I am a failure" or "I am not good enough." Self-labeling can have a significant impact on your self-esteem and emotional health, as it shapes the way you perceive yourself and your abilities. Avoiding self-labeling is necessary to prevent further damage to an already injured soul. In my book "Level Up: Gaining Power During the Fight," I discussed in depth the impact of unaddressed emotional wounds on the soul. An unhealed soul contributes to a disconnect from the Spirit of God which then allows our flesh to rule and keep us in bondage to sin, hurt, shame, and pain. Making it easy for satan to suggest his lies and manipulate us into believing what he is saying about us, and our situations are true. Such deception contributes to us making unwise, unhealthy choices that add to our already broken state or keeps us blind to our need to heal.

Avoiding self-labeling is vital for your emotional well-being. When you label yourself with negative terms or define yourself according to conditions, it can lead to self-fulfilling prophecies, limiting your potential and self-esteem. These labels can become burdens you carry, hindering personal growth and happiness. Instead, you should embrace a mindset of growth, self-acceptance and healing, acknowledging that you are not defined by your past or your challenges. By avoiding self-labeling, you and I open the door to self-discovery, healing, and the opportunity to evolve beyond our perceived limitations, ultimately leading to better emotional stability and health and a more positive self-image.

"If any man is in Christ, he is a new creature, old things have passed away, all things have become new – 2 Corinthians 5:17. God knew just how much pressure to apply to get me to die to self. The process is uncomfortable. Yet, I am learning how to pray more, better, deeper, and stronger. I was forced to sit and be still. I used the time to yield to Him. He healed me and rebuilt me at the same time. In His perfect timing, He restored me.

April 4, 2019, was my exodus. I am still under construction, but I can already feel, see, and hear the changes. I will not rush my healing and renewal process. I will wait on the Lord. Just as I am experiencing my exodus and God's restoration and redemption, you can have your experience as well. My challenge to you is to do it by choice and not by force.

Say goodbye to the old you and embrace the new and improved you. Ask God what baggage you need for Him to claim from you. Ask Him to reveal the emotional damage and help you break free from the chains and shackles. Petition for Him to stop the rollercoaster of emotions and to give you strength to walk free and upright. Request for the strength to make a loud noise and sound the trumpet for the wall to fall. Ask Him to make plain the new changes and how to apply them so you can, not only operate in your divine purpose but do it as your authentically healed self. Once you have decided to give your entire life to Christ, including ALL your junkie junk, leaving nothing but what He is giving you, then you will be free and shall live. To maintain your new life, walk and live in the Spirit (see Galatians 5:25). Watch out! Your greater is coming, and so is mine.

Say hello to the healed you,

Dr. Latoshia

PS. Live on purpose and with love. At the beginning of my healing process, I focused on being intentional about demonstrating at least two attributes from the fruit of the Spirit, which is love, joy, peace, longsuffering, kindness, goodness, faithfulness, gentleness, and self-control (Galatians 5:22). Embrace your God-given uniqueness. He will rebuild your self-esteem, self-respect, and your integrity. The enemy tried it. He tried to change our destiny through pain, suffering, negative situations, experiences, events, manipulation of the truth, and deceit, but God. He can and will restore us to wholeness as if events never happened. That which was meant to take us out can be used to transform us into the person God designed us to be. I encourage you to "Be strong and of good courage" – Joshua 1:9. Focus on the here and now and the plans God has for your life. Let the past be the past. It is already gone. Learn from it. Heal from it and move forward. Your life depends on it. Learn to feel-deal-heal and live a life filled with joy, peace, and the unconditional love of Christ. It is time to live a healed life and thrive. You got this! Say goodbye to the unhealed you. Choose to feel-deal-heal.

Song: "Deliver Me" by Donald Lawrence feat. Le'Andria Johnson

Go to the Feel-Deal-Heal Journal and complete the writing prompt for LOL #40.

"*God knew just how much pressure to apply to get me to die to self.*

The process is uncomfortable.

Yet, I am learning how to pray more, better, deeper, and stronger."

FINAL LOVE NOTE

"Therefore, humble yourselves under the mighty hand of God that
He may exalt you in due time" – Peter 5:6-7.

As I close the chapters of "Feel-Deal-Heal: Acquiring LOVE - Liberty Over Vulnerable Emotions," let us reflect on the profound truth that God, in His boundless love, offers beauty for ashes. He is a healing God, a compassionate presence who cares for us with immeasurable tenderness. His desire is for His children to be healthy, whole, and flourishing in the fullness of emotional well-being.

In the pages of this book, we have journeyed through the imperfections of our world, surrounded by imperfect individuals making choices that contribute to emotional injuries and pain, to include our own choices. It is within this reality that we must choose to heal. God, the ultimate Healer, invites us to release the ashes of our past and embrace the beauty He intends for our present and future.

The letters within "Feel-Deal-Heal" serve as gentle prompts, guiding us to an awareness of the barriers we hold onto – those hurdles that obstruct our path to healing and emotional intelligence. These letters are a testament to the power of self-awareness, prompting us to recognize and release the wrong thinking that impact our emotions that bind us, preventing us from extending love both to ourselves and to others and embracing our need to heal and move forward in a thriving manner.

Our thoughts have a profound effect on how we feel. Negative thoughts about life events can impede our growth, hinder healing, and prevent us from moving forward in a positive and healthy manner. By recognizing these harmful thoughts and aligning them with God's truth, we unlock the path to freedom, enabling us to fee-deal-heal. Embrace the transformative power to aligning your thoughts with God's truth for a liberated and healthier journey forward.

May the lessons gleaned from these pages become a source of inspiration and strength as you navigate the journey ahead. Remember, healing is a choice, and it is a choice worth making. Let the love and care of a healing God guide you towards emotional freedom and fulfillment. As you close this book, embrace the liberty and love that awaits you on the path to "Feel-Deal-Heal." May your heart be lightened, your spirit uplifted, and your journey toward emotional well-being be abundantly blessed.

Stay Kingdom focused and grow in love,

Dr. Latoshia

MASS DEPARTURE

I was knocked down and left to drown in my own sorrow.

But now, I shall live because Jesus holds tomorrow.

I'm letting go of strongholds that have threatened my
lifetime and time again.

I'm dropping the load so that I can let the Holy Spirit abide within.

I'm dropping all baggage and receiving all of God's gifts He has given me.

I once carried failure, but now I have the gift of forgiveness.

I once carried fear, but now I have the gift of freedom.

I once carried guilt, but now I have the gift of grace.

I once carried hate, but now I have the gift of hope.

I once carried jealousy, but now I have the gift of Jesus.

I once carried rejection, but now I have the gift of respect.

I once carried pain, but now I have the gift of purpose.

I once carried shame, but I have the gift of salvation.

Because of the new things, I can walk in light. Walk in love.
Walk in wisdom.

This is my exodus.

Dr. Latoshia

QUICK REFERENCE

STAR

Stop: Don't move or say anything

Think: consider what you are about to say or do and the consequences

Acknowledge: recognize your current feelings.

Respond: act in response to the situation with an informed decision and not an emotional reaction.

WEAPONS OF SPIRITUAL WARFARE

- Praise
- Scripture
- Prayer
- Spiritual songs and Hymns
- Worship
- Fasting
- Feel-Deal-Heal Process

DAILY COPING SKILLS

*Assist with mood stabilization and increase healthy mental and emotional wellness:

Prayer	Self-reflection	Deep breathing	Exercise
Mediation	Positive self-talk	Positive praying	Reading
Writing/ journaling	Eating healthy	Yoga	Listening to music
Singing	Dancing	Rest	Laughter

Reaction: is impulsive; using the emotional brain

Response: is rational/ logical; using the thinking brain.

Feel-Deal-Heal Process

Feel: (Recognize and experience emotions.) The identification, recognition, and experience of emotions. It involves being aware of and acknowledging the various emotions that arise within oneself, whether they are positive, negative, or neutral. Recognizing and accepting one's feelings is an essential aspect of emotional intelligence and self-awareness.

Deal: (Address and manage emotions healthily.) Involves actively engaging with and addressing one's emotions healthily and constructively. It encompasses strategies for coping with difficult emotions, such as stress, anxiety, sadness, or anger. Dealing with emotions may involve techniques such as problem-solving, communication, seeking support from others, and practicing self-care to manage and navigate emotional challenges effectively.

Heal: (Recover and find peace from emotional pain.) The process of recovering and finding resolution from emotional pain, trauma, or distress. It involves actively working towards emotional healing and inner peace, often through self-reflection, self-compassion, and forgiveness. Healing may encompass various approaches, including therapy, mindfulness, self-care practices, and building resilience, as individuals seek to release past hurts, cultivate emotional well-being, and restore a sense of wholeness

VULNERABLE VS NEGATIVE EMOTIONS

Vulnerable emotions can be considered a subset of negative emotions, as they often contribute to the overall experiences of emotional distress. Understanding and navigating these emotions can contribute to emotional healing and well-being.

VULNERABLE	NEGATIVE
Insecurity	Sadness
Fragility	Anger
Fearfulness	Fear
Sensitivity	Insecurity
Shame	Shame
Anxiety	Guilt
Loneliness	Loneliness
Apprehension	Disappointment
Worry	Frustration
Doubt	Anxiety
Helplessness	Envy
Rejection	Resentment
Self-Consciousness	Regret
Isolation	Jealousy
Embarrassment	Powerlessness
Discomfort	Discouragement
Self-Doubt	Despair
Nervousness	Irritation

SOS
Surviving Off Scriptures

These are some of the Scriptures that I am using to stay focused on Christ and increase my faith as I heal and wait for Him to restore me.

Genesis 50:20	Exodus 14:13	Deuteronomy 31:6
Joshua 1:9	Psalm 9:9	Psalm 19:14
Psalm 46:1	Psalm 50:15	Psalm 51
Psalm 54:17	Psalm 107:19	Psalm 118:1, 6
Psalm 119:10-11	Psalm 121	Psalm 124:8
Psalm 126:5-6	Proverbs 3:5-6	Ecclesiastes 1:9
Ecclesiastes 3:1-8	Ecclesiastes 4:9-12	Ecclesiastes 7:21
Ecclesiastes 12:13-14	Isaiah 40:31	Isaiah 41:10, 13
Jeremiah 29:11	Luke 1:37	Luke 18:27
John 1:19	John 14:1, 27	John 15:7
John 16:33	Roman 3:1-5	Romans 8:31
2 Corinthians 5:7	2 Corinthians 12: 9-10	Galatians 5:22-26
Ephesians 3:20	Philippians 1:6	Philippians 3:13-14
Philippians 4:6-9, 13, 19	Colossians 3:2	2 Timothy 1:6-7
Hebrews 4:16	James 1:2-6	1 Peter 5:6-7

Other books and journals:

- ❖ Level Up: Gaining Strength During the Fight
- ❖ A Mother's Prayer: Journal for Incarcerated Mothers
- ❖ A Prayer for Mom: Journal for Teens with Incarcerated Mothers

Journals written under the pen name Love Nelson:

- ❖ Kingdom Teen: True Royalty Journal
- ❖ Notebook
- ❖ Kingdom Man
- ❖ Authentic
- ❖ Know Thy Self

All journals are available on Amazon.

Contact:

Email: dr.lsdaniels@gmail.com

Instagram: Dr. Latoshia